Comfort Food

Comfort
Food

Over 175 tried-and-tested recipes and ideas
for reassuringly satisfying fare

Published by
BBC Worldwide Ltd,
Woodlands, 80 Wood Lane,
London W12 OTT

Designed and produced by
Quadrille Publishing Limited,
Alhambra House,
27–31 Charing Cross Road,
London WC2H OLS

First published 2003
Text © BBC Worldwide and the contributors 2003
Photography © BBC Worldwide and the photographers 2003
(For a full list of contributors and photographers see pages 140-41.)
Original material, design & layout © 2003 Quadrille Publishing
Limited.

ISBN 0 563 48849 2

Editor & Project Manager: **Lewis Esson**
Editorial Director: **Jane O'Shea**
Creative Director: **Helen Lewis**
Design Assistant: **Katy Davis**
Project Editor for the BBC: **Sarah Emsley**
Production: **Nancy Roberts**

Printed in China.

Throughout the book recipes are for four people unless
otherwise stated.
Both metric and imperial quantities are given. Use either all
metric or all imperial, as the two are not necessarily interchangeable.

Contents

Introduction

Even the phrase 'comfort food' is reassuring, reminiscent of tea and toast on rainy afternoons, chicken soup when you're feeling poorly and families sitting round the table tucking in to a fragrantly steaming pie or glistening roast. When we are exhausted by overwork or over-partying, or worn down by winter, tired of transport that fails us, or just feeling plain wronged by life, we want something that's easy to eat, preferably just with a spoon or a fork. Softness is an essential component of comfort: a squidgy, freshly baked loaf, steaming pasta, buttery mashed potatoes, or a lovely creamy pudding.

True comfort food usually consists of those dishes redolent of childhood security, be it mum's cooking or special treats. It can be a function of the way they look or their evocative smell, or even the way their names sound. In general, they do tend to be dishes that have been cooked long and slow to produce lots of enticing odours and flavours, and a texture that is meltingly tender. They are also essentially simple – no layered towers, pictures on plates or sugar cages here. It's basically good, plain, simple food – hearty home cooking like your grandmother used to make.

Familiarity is crucial – nobody craves fusion food when the world looks grim. There is an essential wholesomeness to comfort food, a reliable friendliness that never fails to deliver. It is food that you never really mind taking the time to cook for yourself, and that you can safely serve to family and friends at almost any time, sure in the knowledge that it will elicit nothing but total appreciation.

Rainy day snacks

and suppers

ON THOSE DRAB DAYS WHEN MEALS OFFER THE BEST

CONSOLATION, THE NURSERY ELEMENTS OF COMFORT

FOOD REALLY COME INTO PLAY, WITH THE MELTINGLY

APPEALING JOYS OF BUTTER, CREAM, CHEESE AND EGGS

IN ALL THEIR GUISES TO THE FORE. THESE ARE OFTEN

COMBINED WITH THE HUMBLE BUT ALWAYS SATISFYING

POTATO, BE IT MASHED, DEEP-FRIED OR BAKED.

tartiflette

Tartiflette is what everyone tucks into after a hard morning's skiing down the slopes in France's Haute-Savoie region, but it will cheer anyone up, any day, at any time, in any climate. This is essentially a disgraceful dish, oozing cream and melting cheese between layers of potato and flecks of bacon, but don't let that stop you enjoying every last mouthful.

Preparation 35-40 minutes
Cooking 10-12 minutes

25g/1oz butter, plus more for greasing
750g/1³⁄4lb potatoes
salt and pepper
1 onion
drizzle of olive oil
6 rashers of smoked back bacon
250g/9oz Reblochon or Pont l'Évêque
   cheese
about 150ml/¹⁄4 pint single cream

1 Preheat the oven to 220°C/425°F/Gas 7 and butter a 1.5 litre/2³⁄4 pint ovenproof dish. Peel the potatoes and thickly slice them, then boil in salted water for 8-10 minutes, until just tender. Drain.

2 Chop the onion finely and fry in the 25g/1oz butter with a drizzle of olive oil for 5 minutes. Snip the bacon into pieces with scissors and add to the pan. Stir well and cook for a further 5 minutes, until the onion and bacon are lightly coloured.

3 Chop the cheese into chunks, rind and all. Layer half the potatoes in the prepared dish and scatter over half each of the onion, bacon and cheese. Lightly season with salt and pepper. Repeat the layers, then pour cream evenly over the top.

4 Bake for 10-12 minutes until golden. Let it rest for 5 minutes and then serve it with a salad.

buttery potato cake

This is cosy winter food par excellence. *Not only does it make a deliciously satisfying accompaniment to almost anything else, especially roast meats, but it can be a perfect lunch or supper dish with a salad, and simply tucking into it on its own will raise even the bleakest of spirits.*

Serves 6
Preparation 10 minutes
Cooking 1 hour 15 minutes

50g/2oz butter
1.25kg/2³⁄4lb floury potatoes, such as
   Maris Piper or King Edward's
salt and pepper

1 Preheat the oven to 190°C/375°F/Gas 5 and, using some of the butter, liberally grease a 20-23cm/8-9in cake tin or charlotte mould (it should not be loose-bottomed).

2 Thinly slice the potatoes. Arrange in the base of the tin, season and dot with a few small pieces of butter. Keep layering the potatoes as evenly as you can, seasoning and dotting with butter as you go. Finish with butter and seasoning.

3 Cover the tin with a piece of foil and bake for 45 minutes, then remove the foil and bake for a further 30-45 minutes, until the potatoes are tender when pierced with the tip of a knife.

4 Leave the potato cake to cool in the tin for 5 minutes, then invert on to a serving plate. Serve cut into wedges.

Preparation 25 minutes
Cooking time 1 hour 20 minutes

1 tbsp vegetable oil
2 onions, chopped
450g / 1lb lean minced lamb or beef
2 tsp plain flour
2 carrots, peeled and finely chopped
2 tbsp tomato purée
2 tbsp Worcestershire sauce
$^{1}/_{2}$ tsp dried thyme
$^{1}/_{2}$ tsp dried rosemary
300ml / $^{1}/_{2}$ pint beef or vegetable stock
salt and pepper
1 kg / 2$^{1}/_{4}$lb floury potatoes, peeled
25g / 1oz butter
5 tbsp milk

shepherd's pie

This is one of those humble but totally satisfying dishes that were at one time usually made with leftovers, most usually on a Monday from the remnants of the Sunday lunchtime roast, so it has all those great associations of washday and the smell of clean sheets airing in front of a roaring fire.

1 Heat the oil in a large pan and fry the onions for 7 minutes, until softened and lightly browned. Stir in the lamb or beef and fry until crumbly and evenly browned. Stir in the flour, then the carrots, tomato purée, Worcestershire sauce, herbs and stock. Season, bring to the boil, cover and simmer for 30 minutes, stirring occasionally, until the meat is tender. If the mixture seems dry, add a little water.

2 Meanwhile, chop the potatoes and cook them in a large pan of boiling salted water until tender. Drain, return to the pan, cover and leave to steam. Then dry in the heat (with the lid off) for 5 minutes. Preheat the oven to 200°C/400°F/Gas 6.

3 Remove the lid and mash the potatoes until they are smooth. Mash in the butter and add plenty of salt and pepper, and then beat in the milk.

4 Tip the minced meat mixture into a 1.7 litre/3 pint ovenproof dish. Put spoonfuls of mash over the top, then smooth with a fork, sealing in the filling.

5 Bake for 30-35 minutes until the top of the pie is crisp and golden.

gratin dauphinois

This rather luxurious haute cuisine *treatment of the humble potato is possibly among the most addictive foods known.*

Serves 6-8
Preparation 15 minutes
Cooking 1 hour 10 minutes

butter, for greasing
600ml/1 pint milk
1kg/2¹/₄lb floury potatoes
300ml/¹/₂ pint double cream
salt and pepper
large pinch of freshly grated nutmeg
85g/3oz Gruyère cheese, grated

1 Preheat the oven to 180°C/350°F/Gas 4 and lightly grease a medium-sized baking dish. Pour the milk into a heavy-based pan. Peel the potatoes, cut them into 5mm/¹/₄in thick slices and add at once to the pan of milk so they don't discolour. Bring them to the boil and simmer for 15-20 minutes until almost tender (potatoes take longer to cook in milk than in water).

2 Pour the cream into the pan with the potatoes and milk. Season to taste with salt, pepper and nutmeg, then just bring to the boil. Spoon the potato mixture into the prepared baking dish and sprinkle the top with grated cheese.

3 Bake for 30-40 minutes until the gratin is piping hot and browned on top. Serve straight from the dish.

smoked salmon and haddock fish pie

Serves 8
Preparation 25 minutes
Cooking 40 minutes

25g/1oz butter
3 leeks, sliced
4 tbsp plain flour
½ tsp ground turmeric
900g/2lb skinless haddock fillet,
    cut into large chunks
300g/10oz smoked salmon, cut
    into strips
1 tbsp chopped capers (optional)
3 tbsp chopped fresh dill
grated zest and juice of 1 lemon
about 300ml/½ pint double cream
salt and pepper
3x450g/1lb packets ready-made
    colcannon or 1.35kg/4lb well-seasoned
    mashed potato
450g/1lb cooked green beans or peas, to
serve

Using ready-made colcannon speeds up the making of this fish pie. If you can't find any, though, just use mashed potatoes, which you can flavour with cooked onions, spring onions or cooked shredded cabbage if you like.

1 Preheat the oven to 200°C/400°F/Gas 6. Melt the butter in a large flameproof casserole dish or roasting tin. Tip in the leeks and gently cook for 3-4 minutes until softened, stirring often.

2 Mix the flour and turmeric in a bowl. Toss the haddock pieces in the flour mix, then add to the casserole dish. Fry for 3-4 minutes until golden. Remove from the heat.

3 Scatter the smoked salmon strips over the haddock with the capers, dill and the lemon zest and juice. Pour over the cream and season with a little salt and plenty of ground black pepper. Spoon the colcannon or mashed potato on top.

4 Bake for 25-30 minutes until the topping is golden. Serve with some steamed green beans or peas.

Variation
You can use cod or any other plump white fish instead of the haddock.

fish and pea frittata

If you can't find a ready-made watercress or dill and lemon sauce, make a white sauce as described on page 35 and use that instead. You can leave the cheese in or omit it and flavour the sauce instead with puréed watercress, rocket or spinach, or some chopped dill, lemon juice and grated zest.

Preparation 10 minutes
Cooking 45 minutes

675g/1½lb skinless cod or haddock fillets
100g/4oz frozen peas
200g/7oz fresh watercress or dill and
    lemon sauce
salt and pepper
3 thick slices of bread
25g/1oz butter, melted
85g/3oz mature Cheddar cheese, grated

1 Preheat the oven to 190°C/375°F/Gas 5. Cut the fish into chunks and transfer to a pie dish. Sprinkle over the peas, then pour over the sauce and stir lightly, seasoning to taste if necessary.

2 Cut the bread into cubes and toss with the melted butter. Spread over the pie filling and sprinkle with the cheese.

3 Bake for about 45 minutes until the topping is crisp and the fish is tender.

Makes 4
Preparation 25 minutes
Cooking 15 minutes

100g/4oz white breadcrumbs
2 eggs
450g/1lb potatoes, peeled
450g/1lb smoked haddock
grated zest of 1 lemon
2 tbsp chopped fresh parsley
salt and pepper
flour, for dusting
3 tbsp vegetable oil, for frying

for the tartare sauce
200g/7oz mayonnaise
2 small gherkins, chopped
2 tbsp capers, roughly chopped
1 small shallot, very finely chopped
1 tsp horseradish sauce
1/2 tsp dry or made mustard
2 tbsp finely chopped fresh parsley

fish cakes with tartare sauce

1 Make the tartare sauce: mix all the ingredients and chill (you won't need it all; leftovers keep for 3-4 days, covered, in the fridge and enliven any seafood dish).

2 Preheat the oven to 150°C/300°F/Gas 2. Spread the crumbs over a baking sheet and dry in the oven for 10-15 minutes until pale golden, stirring halfway.

3 At the same time, hard-boil one of the eggs. Cut the potatoes into chunks. Cook in boiling salted water for 10-15 minutes until tender. Drain well and mash with a fork.

4 While the egg and potatoes are cooking, put the fish in a frying pan with just enough water to cover. Bring to the boil, reduce the heat, cover and simmer for about 5 minutes until just cooked. Remove the fish with a palette knife and put on a plate. When it is cool enough to handle, carefully remove the skin and any bones. Flake the fish.

5 Shell the egg and chop it. Carefully mix with the potato, fish, lemon zest, parsley, 1/2 tsp salt and some black pepper. With floured hands, shape into 4 round cakes. Beat the other egg in a shallow bowl. Coat each cake in the egg, then the dried breadcrumbs. Reshape if necessary.

chunky chips with taleggio cheese

Chips and cheese... most people's idea of armchair paradise!

1 Preheat the oven to 200°C/400°F/Gas 6. Cut the baking potatoes into wedges and put in a roasting tin. Drizzle over the olive oil and mix.

2 Bake for 45 minutes, turning the chips halfway through.

3 Cut the Taleggio into strips. When the chips are cooked, top with the cheese, then return to the oven for 3 minutes until the cheese has melted.

4 Serve immediately, seasoned with salt, pepper and a dash of Worcestershire sauce.

Serves 1-2
Preparation 10 minutes
Cooking about 50 minutes

3 baking potatoes
3 tablespoons olive oil
85g/3oz Taleggio cheese
salt and pepper
dash of Worcestershire sauce

lamb, aubergine and spinach lasagne

Serves 8
Preparation 50 minutes
Cooking 45–50 minutes

6 tbsp olive oil
1 onion, finely chopped
1 large carrot, finely chopped
85g/3oz pancetta or bacon, chopped
2 garlic cloves, finely chopped
400g/14oz lean minced lamb
2 sprigs of fresh rosemary or 1 tsp dried
2 bay leaves
300ml/¹/₂ pint tomato passata
150ml/¹/₄ pint red wine or lamb stock
salt and pepper
2 large aubergines, cut into 1cm/¹/₂in
* slices*
500g/1lb 2oz fresh spinach
freshly grated nutmeg
9–12 sheets of fresh lasagne

for the sauce
50g/2oz butter
40g/1¹/₂oz plain flour
700ml/1¹/₄ pints milk
1 bay leaf
50–85g/2–3oz Parmesan cheese, freshly
* grated, plus 2 tbsp for sprinkling*
freshly grated nutmeg

1 Heat 2 tablespoons of oil in a large heavy pan over medium heat. Add the onion, carrot and pancetta or bacon. Sauté for 5–6 minutes, until the onion begins to brown. Add the garlic and cook for 1 minute. Turn up the heat, add the lamb and fry for 10 minutes until it browns, breaking it up with a spatula. Stir in the rosemary, bay, passata and wine or stock. Cook gently, uncovered, for 30–35 minutes or until thick, stirring frequently. Season. Preheat oven to 190°C/375°F/Gas 5.

2 Preheat the grill. Lay the aubergines on a baking sheet, brush with the remaining oil and grill for about 4 minutes each side, until golden. Drain on kitchen paper.

3 Pack the rinsed spinach into a pan, cover and put over high heat until it wilts, stirring occasionally. Drain and press out excess water. Chop roughly, season and add a little nutmeg.

4 Make the sauce: put the butter, flour and milk into a pan and whisk over a medium heat until boiling. Add the bay leaf and cook very gently, stirring, for 10 minutes. Remove the bay. Add the Parmesan, season and add a little nutmeg.

5 Spoon half the lamb into a large ovenproof dish, then half the aubergines, followed by a layer of lasagne, the spinach and half the sauce, then another layer of lasagne, the remaining lamb, aubergines, lasagne and sauce. Sprinkle over the reserved Parmesan and bake for 45–50 minutes, or until bubbling and browned on top. Leave to stand for 10 minutes before serving. Serve with a salad and some crusty bread.

ham and egg stuffed marrow

Preparation 15 minutes
Cooking 20–25 minutes

1 marrow, about 1.5kg/3¹/₄lb
25g/1oz butter, cut into cubes
salt and pepper
6 tbsp ready-made tomato pasta sauce
about 10 slices of wafer-thin ham
4 eggs
85g/3oz Cheddar cheese, grated

1 Preheat the oven to 190°C/375°F/Gas 5. Peel the marrow and halve it, then scoop out the seeds. Put it in a shallow microwave and ovenproof dish, dot with butter and sprinkle with salt and pepper. Cover with microwave-proof film, pierce several times and cook on High for 7 minutes, until tender. (If you don't have a microwave, bake it in the preheated oven for 30–40 minutes until just tender.)

2 Spoon the sauce into the cavity of each marrow half, then arrange the ham on top. Break in the eggs and sprinkle with the cheese. Bake for 12–15 minutes until the eggs are softly set and the cheese has melted and turned golden.

ham, spinach and brie pizza

Preparation about 20 minutes
Cooking 20 minutes

1 tbsp oil
100g/4oz butter, plus more for greasing
2 onions, cut into thin wedges
4 rounded tbsp cranberry sauce
175g/6oz frozen leaf spinach, defrosted
350g/12oz self-raising flour
1/2 tsp salt
175–200ml/6–7fl oz milk
175g/6oz cooked ham as a large thick
  slice, cut into chunks
150g/5oz Brie cheese, sliced

1 Preheat the oven to 220°C/425°F/Gas 7. Heat the oil and 25g/1oz of the butter in a frying pan and fry the onions for 4-5 minutes until golden. Remove from the heat and stir in the cranberry sauce. Set aside.

2 Tip the spinach into a sieve, then use the edge of a plate to press out as much excess moisture as possible.

3 Tip the flour and salt into a bowl. Add the remaining butter and lightly rub with your fingers to make fine breadcrumbs. Stir in enough milk to make a soft dough. Grease a large baking sheet and roll the dough out into a rectangle about 30x23cm/12x9in. Put on the baking sheet.

4 Spread the onion and cranberry mixture over the pizza base, almost to the edges, then scatter over the ham, then the spinach, followed by the Brie.

5 Bake for 15 minutes until the base is golden and crisp.

spiced rice with prawns

Preparation about 10 minutes
Cooking about 10 minutes

200g/7oz long-grain rice
175g/6oz frozen peas
2 tbsp oil, plus a drop extra
1 onion, chopped
3 rashers of streaky bacon, chopped
1 tbsp curry paste or curry powder
250g/9oz peeled cooked tiger prawns,
  defrosted if frozen
1 egg, beaten
soy sauce, to serve (optional)

1 Tip the rice into a pan of boiling salted water and simmer for 10 minutes, adding the peas for the last 3 minutes. Drain.

2 While the rice cooks, heat the oil in a large frying pan or wok, add the onion and bacon and stir-fry for 2–3 minutes until golden. Add the curry paste or powder and stir for a few seconds, then tip in the prawns and stir for 1 minute.

3 Push the prawn mixture to one side of the pan and add the drop of oil to the other side. Pour the egg into the oil, stir until cooked like scrambled eggs, then mix into the prawns.

4 Add the rice and peas, and mix well. Serve immediately, with soy sauce for sprinkling, if you like.

Variations
Use chopped cooked ham instead of prawns, or chopped green beans instead of the peas.

Instead of prawns, chop 2 skinless boneless chicken breasts and cook in the oil until they start to go golden, then add the onion and bacon and continue as above.

swift soothers

There are times when the need for comfort really won't wait, and the mood is so despondent that you are totally disinclined to get involved in long and complex preparation, so here are a few recipes that will deliver more or less instant gratification. The sweet potato chips do, of course, demand lengthy cooking, but only minutes in the kitchen – leaving plenty of time for a nice hot bath and your favourite soap while you wait.

sausages with quick onion gravy and sweet potato chips

If you can't find ready-made onion marmalade, just slice one or two big Spanish onions thinly and cook the slices very gently in a little olive oil and melted butter over a gentle heat, stirring from time to time, for about 40 minutes. Stir in a spoonful or two of balsamic or sherry vinegar, season with black pepper and cook for 10 minutes more.

Preparation 5 minutes
Cooking 40-45 minutes
Ready in 50 minutes

2 large orange sweet potatoes, about
   800g/1³/4lb total weight
3 tbsp vegetable oil
8 plump sausages
365g/12oz jar of onion marmalade
salt

1 Preheat the oven to 200°C/400°F/ Gas 6. Cut the sweet potatoes into wedges and put them in a large roasting tin. Drizzle over 2 tablespoons of the oil and toss the wedges to coat. Roast for 40-45 minutes until cooked through and crisp.
2 Halfway through this cooking time, heat the remaining oil in a frying pan. Add the sausages and cook for 20 minutes, turning regularly until cooked through.
3 Drain off any fat and add the onion marmalade, with about 100ml/3¹/2fl oz water. Stir well, then heat through.
4 Sprinkle the chips with a little salt and serve with the sausages and gravy.

Moroccan lamb burgers

Spicy harissa is the traditional North African accompaniment to couscous and can be found in lots of good delis and better supermarkets, in bottles, tubes and cans. It is invaluable for giving a chilli/garlic kick and cumin/caraway flavour to lots of things, like this mayonnaise.

Serves 6
Preparation 15 minutes
Cooking 10 minutes

1 onion, roughly chopped
2.5cm/1in piece of fresh root ginger,
   peeled and chopped
2 garlic cloves
bunch of fresh coriander or parsley
2 tsp each ground cumin and coriander
1 tsp ground cinnamon
100g/4oz ready-to-eat apricots, finely
   chopped
700g/1¹/2lb lean minced lamb
salt and pepper
oil, for greasing

6 Middle-Eastern-style bread rolls, or
　other rolls of your choice
8 tbsp mayonnaise
2 tsp harissa paste (see left)
lettuce, tomato and cucumber slices, to
　serve

1 Preheat a hot grill, griddle pan or
barbecue. Put the onion, ginger, garlic
and coriander or parsley in a food
processor and whiz until finely
chopped. Add the spices, apricots,
lamb and plenty of salt and pepper,
then pulse until just mixed – do not
overmix as it's best to keep the
mixture slightly chunky. Shape into 6
burgers, keeping them separate with
squares of greaseproof paper or foil.
2 When the grill, griddle pan or
barbecue is hot, put the burgers
straight on to the oiled rack, pan or
grill and cook for 4–5 minutes on each
side.
3 Split the rolls and toast on either or
both sides, depending how you like
them. Mix together the mayonnaise
and harissa.
4 Serve the burgers in the buns with a
little lettuce, tomato and cucumber,
with the spicy mayonnaise on the side.

gnocchi with two cheeses and bacon

*Pre-cooked bacon is quick to use, but
you can cook your own if you prefer.
However, as bacon loses an incredible
amount of water when cooked, you will
need 140g/5oz of uncooked smoked
streaky bacon.*

Preparation 5 minutes
Cooking about 10 minutes

salt
400g/14oz potato gnocchi
5 spring onions
100g/4oz medium-flavoured soft blue
　cheese, such as Dolcelatte
250g/9oz mascarpone cheese
225g/8oz baby spinach
50g/1³/4oz cooked thin and crispy smoked
　streaky bacon
green salad and crusty bread, to serve

1 Bring a pan of salted water to the boil
for the gnocchi. While it heats, slice the
spring onions and blue cheese. Spoon
the mascarpone into a large, deep frying
pan. Add the blue cheese and spring
onions, and leave to melt over a
medium heat, stirring occasionally.
2 Tip the gnocchi into the boiling
water and cook for about 3 minutes,
until they rise to the surface.
3 Add the spinach in large handfuls to
the cheese mixture and stir until just
wilted. Crumble in half the bacon.
4 Skim the gnocchi from the pan with
a draining spoon, stir into the cheese
mixture, then crumble over the
remaining bacon. Serve with salad and
crusty bread.

chilli con carne

Serves 6
Preparation 25-35 minutes, plus
    overnight soaking (optional)
Cooking 2-2^{1}/$_{4}$ hours

250g/9oz dried red kidney beans, or
   2x410g/14oz cans, drained
900g/2lb braising steak
salt and pepper
4 tbsp vegetable oil
2 onions, chopped
^{1}/$_{2}$–1 tsp hot chilli powder or cayenne
   pepper
1 rounded tbsp paprika
1 tbsp cumin seeds
2 tbsp dark muscovado sugar
3 garlic cloves, crushed
900g/2lb ripe tomatoes, skinned and
   roughly chopped
600ml/1 pint beef or chicken stock
soured cream or crème fraîche, to serve
roughly chopped fresh coriander, to serve

The secret of success with this recipe is to fry the beef and onions thoroughly so they are really well caramelized. It is also definitely one of those dishes that taste much better if made well ahead, at least the day before, and reheated.

Traditionally chilli would be served with tortilla chips, chopped onions and grated sharp cheese, usually Monterey Jack, but we can use a mature Cheddar. Alternatively, choose between warmed bread, rice or jacket potatoes, and a leafy salad.

1 If you're using dried beans, put them in a bowl, cover with plenty of cold water and leave them to soak for at least 8 hours, or overnight.

2 Drain the beans, tip them into a pan and cover them with fresh water. Bring to the boil and boil rapidly for 10 minutes. Drain and reserve. If using canned beans, simply drain and rinse.

3 Cut the meat into 1-2cm/^{1}/$_{2}$-^{3}/$_{4}$in cubes, discarding any excess fat. Pat dry on kitchen paper and season with salt and pepper. Heat half the oil in a large, heavy-based saucepan or sauté pan until very hot. Fry half the meat for about 10 minutes or until well browned. Drain with a slotted spoon and set aside. Repeat with the remaining oil and meat.

4 Add the chopped onions to the pan with the chilli, paprika, cumin and sugar, and fry very gently, stirring from time to time, for 8-10 minutes, until deep golden and well caramelized.

5 Return the meat to the pan with the garlic, tomatoes, stock and the kidney beans (if using canned beans, add for only the last 30 minutes of cooking time). Bring to the boil, reduce the heat and simmer, uncovered, on the lowest possible heat for 1^{1}/$_{4}$–1^{1}/$_{2}$ hours, until the meat is meltingly tender.

6 Check the seasoning and serve with spoonfuls of soured cream or crème fraîche and plenty of coriander.

Variations
For a delicious meat-free chilli (chilli *sin carne*), in place of the beef, sauté 2 or 3 diced courgettes,1 large diced aubergine and some diced deseeded sweet peppers (go for different colours) in some oil until just wilting, then proceed as above. You can also ring the changes by using chickpeas, pinto or black beans in place of the red kidney beans.

Preparation about 15 minutes
Cooking about 15–20 minutes

1 tbsp vegetable oil
4 lamb chops or cutlets
small knob of butter
1 onion, thinly sliced
2 tsp plain flour
350ml/12fl oz chicken stock
1 tbsp redcurrant jelly

for the root mash
900g/2lb mixed root vegetables, such as
  potatoes and swede or parsnips and
  carrots, cut into chunks
salt and pepper
3 tbsp milk
25g/1oz butter
1 tbsp chopped fresh thyme or 1 tsp dried

lamb chops with root mash and onion gravy

This eminently soothing plateful is highly adaptable. You could use pork chops and add some apple sauce or mustard in place of redcurrant jelly, and flavour the mash with some sage leaves. Or try sweet potatoes or celeriac for a sophisticated mash.

1 Start the root mash: cook all the vegetables in boiling salted water for 15–20 minutes until tender.

2 Meanwhile, heat the oil in a frying pan. Add the chops, season well with pepper and fry for 5–6 minutes on each side until browned. Remove and keep warm.

3 Drain off all but 2 tablespoons of the fat in the pan, add the knob of butter and heat. Add the onion and fry for 10 minutes until golden brown, stirring often. Stir in the flour and cook for a few seconds until browned. Gradually stir in the stock, stirring, for 1 minute until the gravy has thickened. Stir in the redcurrant jelly until dissolved. Keep warm.

4 Finish the mash: drain the vegetables, then mash with the milk and butter. Stir in the thyme, season well and serve with the chops and gravy.

warm summer bean and sausage salad

Broad beans are one of those great tastes of summer, but such a fiddle to prepare. Thankfully nowadays many better supermarkets are selling these little gems ready podded and skinned. If you can't get any broad beans, try using some nice fresh garden peas instead.

1 Cook the pasta in a large pan of boiling salted water for 10 minutes until tender, then drain well. Cook the broad beans in a separate pan of boiling salted water for about 5 minutes until tender, then drain.

2 While they are cooking, heat 1 tablespoon of the oil in a frying pan. Prick the sausages and cook until nicely browned, about 10-12 minutes. Press down on them with a spatula to squeeze out as much fat as possible. Remove the sausages from the pan and slice at an angle. Set aside with their juices.

3 Slacken the pesto with the remaining oil. Wipe the frying pan with kitchen paper and add the sliced sausages with their juices, the broad beans, cherry tomatoes and pasta. Stir in the pesto until well combined. Warm through and serve.

Preparation 10 minutes
Cooking 20 minutes

250g/9oz dried pasta shapes (shells are best)
salt and pepper
450g/1lb fresh broad beans, podded
2 tbsp olive oil
450g/1lb pork sausages (Toulouse or Italian are best in this recipe)
1 tbsp fresh pesto sauce
250g/9oz cherry tomatoes, quartered

pacifying pies

Pies are synonymous with childhood security and good home-made food. There is something about the combination of hot savoury fillings and crisp buttery pastry that simply cannot be beaten... and as for those bits of pastry that have soaked up some of the gravy in the cooking, the queue begins here!

mixed mushroom and chestnut pies

Preparation 20 minutes
Cooking 30 minutes

25g/1oz butter
2 tbsp olive oil
2 shallots, chopped
3 leeks, about 450g/1lb, sliced
2 garlic cloves, finely chopped
450g/1lb mixed mushrooms, e.g. chestnut, girolle, shiitake, halved if large
4 tbsp sherry
200g/7oz vacuum-packed cooked chestnuts
1 tbsp fresh thyme leaves
2 tbsp chopped fresh parsley
200ml/7fl oz crème fraîche
500g/1lb 2oz puff pastry
flour, for dusting
1 beaten egg, to glaze
pepper
sprigs of fresh thyme, to garnish

1 Melt the butter with a tablespoon of oil in a large frying pan, then cook the shallots, leeks and garlic for 4-5 minutes until starting to brown.
2 Add the remaining oil and the mushrooms, and fry for 5 minutes until the juices just start to run. Over a fairly high heat, stir in the sherry and bubble for 1 minute. Stir in the chestnuts, thyme, parsley and crème fraîche. Spoon into 4 round 300ml/½ pint (13cm/5in) ovenproof dishes and leave to cool.
3 Meanwhile, preheat the oven to 220°C/425°F/Gas 7. Roll the pastry out to just over 5mm/¼in and cut out 4 circles slightly larger than the dishes. Using trimmings, cut out 5mm/¼in wide pastry strips. Brush the dish rims with water and stick the strips round the rims. Brush the strips with water and put the lids on top. Press to seal and knock up edges with the back of a knife.
4 Make a small hole in the centre of each lid with a knife, brush the pastry with egg and sprinkle with freshly ground black pepper. Put the pies on a baking sheet and bake for about 15 minutes, until the pastry is puffed and golden. Garnish with sprigs of thyme.

steak and kidney pie

Serves 6
Preparation 30 minutes
Cooking about 2 hours

1 tbsp vegetable oil
knob of butter
2 onions, roughly chopped
225g/8oz lambs' kidneys, halved, tubes removed, and skinned
700g/1½lb chuck steak, cubed
2 tbsp plain flour
2 bay leaves
leaves from 4 sprigs of fresh thyme
600ml/1 pint beef stock
4 field mushrooms, thickly sliced
1 tsp tomato purée
1 tsp mushroom seasoning or Worcestershire sauce
3 tbsp chopped fresh parsley

for the pastry
175g/6oz butter
225g/8oz plain flour
¼ tsp salt
1 beaten egg, to glaze

1 Heat the oil and butter in a large pan, then fry the onions for 3-4 minutes, stirring. Fry the meat for 2-3 minutes until no longer pink. Stir in the flour and cook for 2 minutes. Add the herbs and stock. Stir until thickened and just at the boil. Add the mushrooms and tomato purée, lower heat and simmer, covered, for about 1¹/₂ hours, until the meat is tender.

2 To make the pastry: wrap the butter in foil and freeze for 45 minutes. In a large bowl, mix the flour with the salt. Holding the frozen butter in a piece of foil, dip it in the flour and grate coarsely into the bowl. Keep dipping the butter in the flour as you grate. Mix in the butter with a knife until evenly coated with flour. Stir in 8-9 tablespoons of water to form a dough. Roll into a ball, wrap in film and chill for 30 minutes.

3 When the meat is cooked, remove the bay, season and add the mushroom seasoning or Worcestershire sauce, then allow to cool slightly. Preheat oven to 200°C/400°F/Gas 6.

4 Roll out pastry to about 5mm/¹/₄in thick and 2.5cm/1in wider than a 1.2 litre/2 pint pie dish. Cut out a lid slightly bigger than the dish. Cut a strip of pastry the width of the rim.

5 Stir the parsley into the meat and transfer to the dish. Brush the rim with egg, then lay the pastry strip around the top and seal. Brush with egg and put the lid on. Seal edges, knock up with the back of a knife and flute. Cut a slit in the lid and brush with egg (not the edges or they won't rise). Bake for 20 minutes, brush with egg again and bake for 10 minutes more.

chicken and ham pie

Serves 6
Preparation 25 minutes
Cooking 40-45 minutes

6 boneless, skinless chicken breasts, cubed
3 carrots, chopped
3 potatoes, peeled and cubed
2 celery stalks, chopped
2 tsp chopped fresh thyme or 1 tsp dried
850ml/1¹/₂ pints hot chicken stock
50g/2oz butter
2 onions, chopped
50g/2oz plain flour
300ml/¹/₂pint milk
juice of 1 lemon
2 tbsp chopped parsley
4 thin slices of ham, cut into strips
500g/1lb 2 oz shortcrust pastry
1 egg, beaten

1 Put the chicken in a large pan with carrots, potatoes, celery, half the thyme and seasoning. Add stock and bring to the boil. Reduce heat, cover and cook gently for 15 minutes. Set a colander over a large bowl, pour in pan contents and remove thyme. Reserve 600ml/1 pint (rest can be frozen).

2 Rinse the pan, return to heat and melt the butter. Cook the onions until soft, about 5 minutes. Stir in the flour, then the reserved stock, a little at a time, to make a smooth thick sauce. Add the milk and simmer for 2 minutes. Off heat, stir in the remaining thyme, lemon juice and parsley. Season.

3 Mix together the chicken, vegetables and ham in a deep 2.2 litre/4 pint ovenproof dish, preferably with a rim or lip. Pour over the sauce and leave to cool slightly. Preheat the oven to 200°C/400°F/Gas 6.

4 Roll out the pastry to about 5cm/2in larger than the top of the dish. Cut a 2.5cm/1in strip from all round pastry. Brush the rim of the dish with egg and press the strip all round. Brush with egg and lift the pastry on to it, pressing the edges to seal thoroughly. Trim off excess, then mark the pastry edge all round with a fork. Make 4 small slits in the centre. Brush with egg and bake for 25-30 minutes until crisp and golden.

Budget
buckers-up

THANKFULLY, COMFORT FOOD IS OFTEN FAIRLY INEXPENSIVE, USING MOSTLY HUMBLE INGREDIENTS LIKE POTATOES, ONIONS, CHEESE AND THAT HERO OF THE HOUR, THE SAUSAGE. CANNED FOODS, LIKE TUNA, BEANS AND CORNED BEEF, ALSO HAVE A ROLE TO PLAY, BEING BOTH CHEAP AND FAST. PASTA, TOO, HAS A FAIRLY UNIQUE POSITION IN PACIFYING FOR PENNIES.

seafood spaghetti

Serves 2
Preparation about 5 minutes
Cooking 10-12 minutes

175g/6oz spaghetti
salt and pepper
1 tbsp olive oil
2 garlic cloves, finely chopped
400g/14oz can of chopped tomatoes
200g/7oz jar of cockles in vinegar,
*   drained*
pinch of dried chilli flakes
2 tbsp chopped fresh parsley

This dish can provide a welcome taste of summer on a winter's evening.

1 Cook the spaghetti in a pan of rapidly boiling salted water for 10-12 minutes until tender.

2 While it is cooking, heat the oil in a frying pan and fry the garlic for 30 seconds. Add the tomatoes and bubble for 2-3 minutes. Add the cockles and chilli flakes, season with salt and pepper, then stir to heat through.

3 Drain the cooked spaghetti and return to the pan. Stir in the sauce and serve sprinkled with chopped parsley.

Variation
If you can't get cockles, use canned clams or mussels.

tuna pasta niçoise

Preparation about 10 minutes
Cooking about 10 minutes

350g/12oz pasta, such as conchiglie,
*   tagliatelle or penne*
salt and pepper
4 tbsp olive oil
1 tbsp lemon juice or white wine vinegar
250g/9oz cherry tomatoes, halved
50g/2oz can of anchovies, drained and
*   chopped*
85g/3oz can of tuna in olive oil, drained
handful of fresh herbs, such as chives,
*   basil, parsley*

The use of mostly storecupboard ingredients makes this perfect for unexpected guests.

1 Tip the pasta into a pan of boiling salted water and stir well, then boil rapidly for 10 minutes or until just tender.

2 While the pasta is cooking, put the oil and the lemon juice or vinegar into a medium microwave-safe bowl. Tip in the tomatoes and anchovies and gently stir to mix with the dressing. Microwave on High for $2-2^{1}/_{2}$ minutes, stirring halfway, until the tomatoes just start to burst and soften. If you don't have a microwave, put the oil and lemon juice or vinegar into a saucepan with the tomatoes and anchovies, and gently stir to mix. Cook over a low heat for 3-4 minutes, stirring once or twice.

3 Drain the cooked pasta and return it to the pan. Break the tuna into rough chunks, then toss into the pasta with the warm tomato and anchovy dressing, and the herbs. Season with black pepper and serve immediately.

Variation
Replace the can of tuna with 100g/4oz peeled cooked prawns.

placating pasta bakes and gratins

Simplicity itself, nothing can beat a piping-hot dish of soothing pasta in an luscious creamy cheesy sauce, baked or grilled until crisp and brown on top. Added flavourings can include sausages, as here, or other inexpensive ingredients like canned tuna or chopped ham or salami. Including something like frozen spinach is a great way to get kids to eat their greens.

cauli-macaroni cheese

Preparation 15 minutes
Cooking 20-25 minutes

salt and pepper
300g/10oz rigatoni, penne or macaroni
1 small cauliflower, separated into florets
200ml/7fl oz crème fraîche
2 tsp wholegrain mustard
175g/6oz Red Leicester cheese, grated
2 tomatoes, cut into wedges

1 Bring a large pan of salted water to the boil. Add the pasta, stir well, bring back to the boil and then cook, uncovered, for a couple of minutes. Tip in the cauliflower florets, bring back to the boil again and cook for a further 8-10 minutes, until both the pasta and the cauliflower are tender but still firm to the bite. Drain well. Preheat a hot grill.
2 Add the crème fraîche, mustard and all but a good handful of the cheese to the pasta pan. Stir over a low heat until the cheese just starts to melt. Tip the pasta and cauliflower into the cheese sauce and gently stir together. Season and transfer to a flameproof dish.
3 Scatter the tomatoes over the top, followed by the rest of the cheese and some pepper. Grill for about 5 minutes until browned and bubbling.

penne with blue cheese sauce

Preparation 5 minutes
Cooking 15-20 minutes

Danish Blue is a bargain among blue cheeses, but Gorgonzola, Dolcelatte or even Stilton will taste better.

salt and pepper
350g/12oz pasta, such as penne
200g/7oz frozen leaf spinach
85g/3oz Danish blue cheese, crumbled
pinch of chilli flakes (optional)
250g/9oz mascarpone cheese
25g/1oz Parmesan cheese, grated

1 Bring a large pan of salted water to the boil. Add the pasta, bring back to a rapid boil and cook for 10-12 minutes until tender but still firm to the bite, adding the spinach to the pan for the last few minutes of cooking time. Preheat a hot grill.
2 Drain the pasta and spinach, then quickly tip them into a shallow heatproof dish along with the Danish blue, chilli flakes if using and plenty of black pepper.
3 Put spoonfuls of the mascarpone over the top of the cooked pasta. Sprinkle with the Parmesan and grill for 5 minutes until the mascarpone melts into a sauce and the Parmesan turns golden brown. Serve with a green salad.

rigatoni sausage bake

Serves 6
Preparation 20 minutes
Cooking 45-50 minutes

400g/14oz good-quality pork sausages
1 tbsp olive oil
1 onion, chopped
1 large carrot, grated
150ml/¼ pint red wine
300ml/½ pint vegetable stock
3 tbsp tomato purée
salt and pepper
500g/1lb 2oz rigatoni or penne
200g/7oz fresh spinach
150g/5oz mature Cheddar cheese, grated

for the white sauce
50g/2oz butter
50g/2oz plain flour
600ml/1 pint milk
freshly grated nutmeg

1 Slit the sausages and remove them from their skins, then chop them into small pieces. Heat the oil in a pan, add the onion and fry for 5 minutes, until softened and lightly browned. Stir in the sausages and fry until lightly coloured. Add the carrot, then stir in the wine, stock, tomato purée and some seasoning. Bring to the boil, then simmer, uncovered, for about 15 minutes until thickened. Taste and adjust the seasoning. Set aside.

2 Preheat the oven to 190°C/375°F/ Gas 5. Bring a large pan of salted water to the boil. Add the pasta, stir well, then boil rapidly, uncovered, for 10-12 minutes, until tender but still firm to the bite. Remove from the heat, stir in the spinach and, when just wilted, drain well.

3 Towards the end of the pasta cooking time, make the sauce. Put the butter, flour and milk in a pan, then gently heat, whisking, until thickened and smooth. Add a sprinkle of freshly grated nutmeg, season and then simmer for 2 minutes.

4 Tip half the drained pasta into a shallow ovenproof dish, about 2.25 litre/4 pints, and level. Spoon over the sausage sauce, then cover with the remaining pasta. Pour the white sauce evenly over the top and sprinkle with the Cheddar. Bake for 20-25 minutes until golden brown. Allow to stand for 5 minutes before serving.

shepherd's pie jackets

Preparation about 10 minutes
Cooking about 25 minutes

4 baking potatoes
450g/1lb minced beef
1 onion, chopped
good splash of Worcestershire sauce
300ml/¹/₂ pint beef stock
1 tbsp tomato purée
salt and pepper
splash of milk
knob of butter
50g/2oz Cheddar cheese, grated

If you haven't got a microwave, you can simply bake the potatoes in an oven preheated to 180°C/350°F/Gas 4 for about an hour.

1 Put the potatoes in the microwave and cook on High for 20 minutes, until cooked through.

2 Meanwhile, cook the mince and onion in a pan for 10 minutes until the onion is golden and the mince has lost its pink colour. Stir in the Worcestershire sauce and cook for 1 minute. Add the stock and tomato purée, then cover and simmer for 20 minutes until the meat is cooked through.

3 When the potatoes are cooked, cut them in half and scoop out the flesh into a bowl, leaving a thin layer. Add some salt and pepper to the flesh, then stir in the milk and butter.

4 Preheat the grill. Put the potato skins in a shallow roasting tin and spoon in the meat mixture. Top with the potato and sprinkle with cheese. Grill until the cheese has melted and the potato filling is hot. Serve with steamed green vegetables.

rumbledethumps

Serves 8
Preparation about 15 minutes
Cooking about 1 hour

1kg/2¼lb potatoes
600g/1lb 5oz neeps (see introduction)
salt and pepper
100g/4oz butter
400g/14oz Savoy cabbage, thinly sliced
50g/2oz Cheddar cheese, grated

This is a variation on a much-loved vegetable dish from the Scottish Borders. Neeps (short for turnips) are what the Scots call swedes.

1 Peel the potatoes and neeps, and chop them, then boil them together in a large pan of salted water for 25–30 minutes until tender.

2 Preheat the oven to 160°C/325°F/Gas 3. Drain the vegetables well, return them to the pan and cover tightly, then shake over a low heat to dry them off completely.

3 Heat half the butter in another pan, add the cabbage and cook until just tender but still bright green (3–4 minutes). Tip all the buttery cabbage into the potato pan and add the remaining butter. Roughly mash everything together and season to taste with salt and pepper.

4 Tip into an ovenproof dish, top with the cheese and bake for 30 minutes.

5 Before serving, preheat the grill and flash the rumbledethumps under the grill for 5 minutes to brown the top.

chicken curry with chickpeas

Preparation 30–40 minutes
Cooking 30 minutes

2 onions, quartered
3 fat garlic cloves
3cm/1¼in piece of fresh root ginger,
*   peeled and roughly chopped*
2 tbsp medium curry powder
½ tsp turmeric
2 tsp paprika
1 fresh red chilli, deseeded and roughly
*   chopped*
1 tsp salt
20g/⅔oz fresh coriander
1 chicken stock cube
450ml/¾ pint boiling water
4 skinless boneless chicken breast fillets
*   (about 500g/1lb 2oz in total), cubed*
410g/14oz can of chickpeas, drained and
*   rinsed*
natural yoghurt, basmati rice, naan bread
*   or grilled poppadums, to serve*

1 Put the onions, garlic, ginger, curry powder, ground spices, chilli, salt and half the coriander into a food processor. Blend to a purée. Tip the mixture into a medium saucepan and cook over a low heat for 10 minutes, stirring frequently.

2 Crumble in the stock cube, add the boiling water and bring back to the boil. Add the cubed chicken, stir well, then lower the heat and simmer for 20 minutes until the chicken is cooked through.

3 Chop the remaining coriander, reserve 2 tablespoons of it and stir the rest into the curry mixture together with the chickpeas. Heat through.

4 Divide between 4 bowls, sprinkle with the reserved coriander and spoon over the yoghurt, then serve with basmati rice, naan bread or poppadums.

chicken with garlic and bay leaves

Preparation 5 minutes
Cooking about 1 hour

8 large chicken thighs
salt and pepper
4 tbsp olive oil
1 large head of garlic, separated into cloves
*   but the skins left on*
8 bay leaves, preferably fresh
250ml/9fl oz dry white wine

1 Season the chicken thighs liberally with salt and pepper.

2 Heat the oil in a large heavy-based frying pan (which has a lid) over a moderate heat. When hot, fry the garlic gently until lightly golden. Remove and set aside.

3 Add half the chicken to the pan and fry briskly for 4–5 minutes until golden all over. Cook the remaining chicken in the same way.

4 Return all the chicken to the pan, with the garlic and bay. Add the wine, shaking the pan to help it emulsify with the oil. Simmer for 3–4 minutes, turning the chicken.

5 Stir in 150ml/¼ pint water, cover and simmer very gently for 30 minutes, or until the chicken is just cooked through, checking from time to time and adding more water if necessary. Adjust the seasoning before serving.

Variation
Stirring in a little double cream just before serving gives a very luxurious finish.

toad-in-the-hole with red onions and thyme batter

Preparation 30-40 minutes
Cooking 40 minutes

*1 red onion, cut into wedges, layers
 separated*
8 thick pork sausages
1 tsp olive oil

for the batter
100g/4oz plain flour
1 medium egg
300ml/½ pint skimmed milk
2 tsp wholegrain mustard
1 tsp fresh thyme leaves
salt and pepper

1 Preheat the oven to 200°C/400°F/Gas 5. Tip the onions into a small shallow non-stick tin (about 23x30cm/9x12in). Arrange the sausages on top of the onions, then trickle over the oil and roast for 20 minutes.

2 While the sausages are roasting, make the batter. Sift the flour into a bowl, drop the egg into the centre and beat in the milk a little at a time until it makes a smooth batter. Stir in the mustard and thyme and season.

3 Pour the batter quickly into the tin and return to the oven for 40 minutes until the batter is risen and golden. Serve with steamed carrots and cabbage.

cheat's moussaka

If you can't find a ready-made cheese sauce, make one as described on page 18 and use that instead.

Preparation about 5 minutes
Cooking 45-50 minutes

1 tbsp olive oil
1 large onion, chopped
500g/1lb 2oz minced pork or lamb
2 tsp dried oregano
2 x 400g/14oz can of chopped tomatoes
salt and pepper
1 aubergine, cubed
300ml/½ pint carton of cheese sauce
2 eggs, beaten

1 Heat the oil and fry the onion for about 5 minutes until softened. Add the mince and fry quickly until evenly browned. Sprinkle in the oregano, then tip in the tomatoes, salt and pepper. Bring to the boil, then stir in the aubergine, cover and simmer for 20 minutes until the aubergine is tender. Preheat the oven to 180°C/350°F/Gas 4.

2 Mix together the cheese sauce and the eggs. Tip the meat into a 1.4 litre/2½ pint ovenproof dish, then pour over the cheese sauce.

3 Bake for 20-25 minutes until lightly set and golden. Leave to cool for 5 minutes, then serve with a green salad.

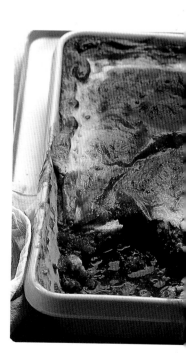

Spanish chicken casserole

Preparation about 15 minutes
Cooking about 45 minutes

3 tbsp olive oil
2 onions, sliced
8 skinless chicken thighs
salt and pepper
1 tbsp plain flour
300ml/ ¹/₂ pint chicken stock
grated zest of 1 orange and juice of 2
   oranges
150ml/ ¹/₄ pint sherry
1 tbsp Worcestershire sauce
300g/10oz button mushrooms, sliced
2 tbsp chopped fresh parsley

1 Heat 2 tablespoons of the olive oil in a large heavy pan, then add the onions and fry for about 10 minutes until lightly browned and soft. Transfer to a plate.

2 Toss the chicken in the seasoned flour. Heat the remaining tablespoon of oil in the pan, then add the chicken and fry until evenly browned. Add the chicken stock, onions and their juices, orange zest and juice, sherry and Worcestershire sauce. Bring to the boil, then reduce the heat, cover and simmer for 25 minutes until the chicken is just cooked through.

3 Stir in the mushrooms and cook for 5 minutes. Taste and season with salt and black pepper if necessary. Just before serving, sprinkle over the chopped parsley and serve with boiled rice.

cowboy casserole

Preparation 15 minutes
Cooking 35-45 minutes

2 medium onions, very thinly sliced
350g/12oz can of lean corned beef or ham
450g/1lb potatoes, sliced and cooked
400g/14oz can of baked beans in
*   tomato sauce*
2 tbsp Worcestershire sauce
large pinch of dried mixed herbs
1 beef stock cube, crumbled
black pepper

1 Preheat the oven to 190°C/375°F/Gas 5. Spread half the onion slices over the base of a 1.75 litre/3 pint casserole. Cut the corned beef or ham into 8 slices and lay 4 on top of the onions. Add half the potatoes to the casserole. Drain the baked beans, reserving the sauce in a measuring jug, then spread them on top of the potatoes. Add the remaining onions, followed by the rest of the corned beef or ham, then arrange the remaining potatoes on top.

2 Add the Worcestershire sauce to the reserved tomato sauce, stir in the herbs, the stock cube and a few twists of black pepper. Make up to 200ml/7fl oz with boiling water and pour over the casserole.

3 Cover and bake for 35-45 minutes, until the onions are cooked. About 10 minutes before the end of the cooking time, remove the lid to allow the potatoes on the top to become brown and crispy. Serve piping hot, with green vegetables.

quick curried kedgeree

Preparation about 15 minutes
Cooking 25 minutes

bunch of spring or salad onions, trimmed
knob of butter
1 tbsp curry powder
400g/14oz basmati rice
700ml/1¼ pints hot chicken or
    vegetable stock
4 eggs
225g/8oz smoked salmon trimmings
salt and pepper

1 Cut the green tops off the onions and roughly chop them, then roughly chop the white parts. Melt the butter in a large saucepan over a medium heat and tip in the white onions and the curry powder. Cook for a few minutes until the onions soften, then tip in the rice and stir to coat in the butter.

2 Pour in the hot stock and bring to the boil. Stir once and boil for 5 minutes, then cover the pan and continue cooking the rice on the lowest possible heat for 15 minutes.

3 While the rice is cooking, bring a small pan of water to simmering point. Lower in the eggs and simmer for 8-9 minutes until soft-boiled. Move the pan to the sink and tip off the hot water, then fill the pan with cold water from the tap. Take out the eggs, then shell and roughly chop them.

4 Tip the rice into a serving dish, toss in the smoked salmon and the green onions and fork through. Taste and add salt and pepper if needed. Put the pieces of egg on top and gently fork them through before serving.

Variation
Use prawns, flaked smoked mackerel, trout or canned tuna instead of smoked salmon.

curried egg rösti

Preparation about 20 minutes
Cooking 20-25 minutes

675g/1¹/₂lb Maris Piper or King
  Edward potatoes, peeled and grated
2 tbsp Madras curry powder, roasted in a
  dry frying pan until aromatic
salt and pepper
3 tbsp olive oil
4 eggs
¹/₂ bunch of spring onions, chopped

This substantial warming supper is all cooked in one pan. Rösti is easy and quick to make at home with grated potatoes, so there is no need to buy expensive ready-made versions from supermarkets.

1 Preheat the oven to 200°C/400°F/Gas 6. Put the grated potato in a clean tea towel and squeeze out as much liquid as possible. Transfer the potato to a large bowl. Add the curry powder, season and mix together.

2 Heat 2 tablespoons of the oil in a large, shallow ovenproof frying pan. Add the mixture, press it down lightly to fill the entire pan and fry over a medium heat for 7-10 minutes until golden underneath.

3 Using a large plate, turn the rösti out, browned side up. Heat the remaining oil in the pan and slide the rösti back into the pan. Make 4 indentations in the top, ready for the eggs. Put in the oven for 5-6 minutes until browned and just cooked.

4 Crack the eggs into the indentations, scatter over the spring onions and cover. Return to the oven for a further 5 minutes until the eggs are just set. Serve at once.

pea, ham and potato omelette

Preparation about 15 minutes
Cooking 40-45 minutes

650g/1lb 7oz potatoes, preferably
red-skinned
6 tbsp olive oil
1 onion, chopped
8 eggs
salt and pepper
150g/5oz ham in a thick slice, cubed
250g/9oz frozen peas

As well as being among the most comforting of foods, omelettes are also the most versatile. Any number of fab fillings are possible, from simple combinations like cheese and tomato to prawn and sautéed mushroom or smoked salmon and cream cheese.

1 Thickly slice the potatoes. Heat 4 tablespoons of the oil in a large flameproof frying pan and fry the potatoes gently for about 15 minutes until they are beginning to turn golden and are just tender when pierced with a knife. Add the onion to the pan and cook for 5 minutes more.

2 In a large bowl, beat the eggs with plenty of salt and pepper. Tip the potatoes, onions, ham and peas into the eggs. Mix gently so you don't break up the potatoes too much.

3 Preheat a hot grill and heat the remaining oil in the pan. Add the egg mixture and gently cook for 10 minutes until half set, then grill for 10-15 minutes until the omelette is golden and just set. Serve cut into wedges.

chilli baked eggs

Preparation about 15 minutes
Cooking 30-35 minutes

2 tbsp olive oil
1 large onion, chopped
2 garlic cloves, crushed
2 green chillies, deseeded and chopped
1/2 tsp ground cumin
one 400g/14oz can and one 200g/7oz
can of chopped tomatoes
1 tbsp tomato paste
2 tbsp chopped fresh coriander or parsley
(optional)
salt and pepper
4 eggs
50g/2oz Gruyère or Cheddar cheese,
coarsely grated
wheat tortillas or thick toast, to serve

This is an adaptation of the classic Spanish and Latin American dish called huevos rancheros *or* cowboy eggs. *You can also simply poach or fry the eggs and pour the chilli sauce over them.*

1 Heat the oil in a large deep frying pan and fry the onion for 5 minutes. Add the garlic, chillies and cumin, and fry for 1 minute. Add the tomatoes and the tomato paste, then simmer for 15 minutes. Add the coriander or parsley, if using, and season to taste.

2 Break 1 egg into a cup, make a hollow in the mixture in the pan and slide the egg into it. Repeat with the other eggs. Sprinkle the whole thing with cheese, cover and simmer for 10-12 minutes, until the eggs are set. Meanwhile, preheat a hot grill.

3 Slide the pan under the grill for 1 minute, until the cheese is lightly golden and bubbling. Serve with the tortillas or toast.

Sunday
uplifters

roast rib of beef with mixed pepper and thyme crust

Serves 6
Preparation 5 minutes
Cooking time 1 hour 35 minutes

piece of boneless rib of beef, about
  2.5kg/5¹/₂lb
2 tbsp mixed peppercorns
2 tbsp fresh thyme leaves
1 tsp coarse sea salt
1 tsp olive oil

for the gravy
1 tbsp plain flour
2 tsp Dijon mustard
600ml/1 pint beef stock

1 Wipe the meat with damp kitchen paper and weigh it. Preheat the oven to 230°C/450°F/Gas 8. Using a mortar and pestle, crush the peppercorns, thyme leaves and sea salt. Brush the oil over the beef and press on the peppercorn and thyme mixture.

2 Roast uncovered for 20 minutes, then lower the oven setting to 190°C/375°F/Gas 5 and roast for another 30 minutes per kg/15 minutes per lb for rare. For medium to well done, cook for an additional 15-25 minutes. When the meat is done, take it out of the roasting tin and leave it to rest.

3 To make the gravy, put the roasting tin on a medium heat on the stove. Stir the flour into the meat juices with a wooden spoon. Cook for 1 minute, then stir in the mustard and pour in the stock. Turn up the heat and bring to the boil, stirring all the time until the gravy has thickened very slightly, then simmer for 1 minute to cook the flour. Serve with the roast beef.

pot-roasted brisket in beer with parsnips and mushrooms

Serves 6-8
Preparation about 30 minutes
Cooking 2¹/₂-3 hours

1–1.25kg/2¹/₄–2³/₄lb boned rolled brisket
salt and pepper
5 tbsp vegetable oil
large knob of butter
2 large onions, halved and sliced
2–3 celery stalks, finely chopped
2 carrots, sliced
200–250g/7–9oz large flat mushrooms,
  stalks chopped and caps thickly sliced
500/18fl oz brown ale or stout
a few fresh thyme sprigs
2 bay leaves
1–2 tsp light muscovado sugar
500g/1lb 2oz parsnips, cut into wedges
1 tbsp Dijon mustard
chopped fresh parsley or thyme, to serve

1 Preheat the oven to 190°C/375°F/Gas 5. Wash and dry the brisket, then season all over. Heat 2 tablespoons of oil in a deep casserole and brown the beef all over. Remove from the pan. Turn down the heat, add the butter and fry the onions, celery, carrots and mushroom stalks for 6-8 minutes. Return the beef to the pan and add the beer, thyme, bay and sugar. Add water, if needed, so that the liquid comes about two-thirds up the beef. Season, bring to a simmer and cover tightly.

2 Cook in the oven for 20 minutes. Reduce the oven setting to 160°C/325°F/Gas 3 and cook for 2 more hours, turning the beef twice, until tender. About an hour before it is due to be done, toss the parsnips in the remaining oil, season and roast on a baking tray above the beef for 50-60 minutes, turning once, until tender.

3 Turn the oven back to 190°C/375°F/Gas 5. Lift out the beef, cover it with foil and keep it warm. Stir the parsnips and mushroom caps into the beef juices. Adjust the seasoning and add a little water if needed. Cover and return to the oven for 20-25 minutes.

4 To serve, use a slotted spoon to remove the vegetables and arrange round the beef. Spoon off the excess fat from the pan juices, then whisk in the mustard and pour into a jug. Moisten the beef with a little of the juices and scatter with herbs.

roast pork with apples, cider vinegar and rosemary

Serves 6-8
Preparation 30 minutes
Cooking time about 2¹/₂ hours, plus
   15 minutes' resting

2–2.25kg/4¹/₂–5lb loin of pork on the
  bone, rind removed
1 garlic clove, crushed
1 tsp finely chopped fresh rosemary, plus a
  few extra whole sprigs
salt and pepper
1 large onion, thickly sliced
2 tbsp cider vinegar, plus extra
  for the gravy
2 tbsp redcurrant jelly, plus extra
  for the gravy
500ml/18fl oz vegetable stock

for the apples
50g/2oz butter
1 small onion, finely chopped
grated zest of 1 small lemon
50g/2oz fresh white breadcrumbs
1 tsp finely chopped fresh rosemary needles
6 good-sized apples, preferably Golden
  Delicious

Cook the rind separately to make crackling – it will crisp better – then coat the joint with a redcurrant glaze. Serve with mash and a seasonal green vegetable.

1 Make some deep incisions in the pork, close to the bone. Mix together the garlic, chopped rosemary and 1 teaspoon salt. Rub into the cuts, spreading any extra over the meat. Set aside for 20 minutes. Meanwhile, preheat oven to 220°C/425°F/Gas 7.

2 Scatter the onion and a few sprigs of rosemary into a roasting tin. Put the pork on top, skinned side up, cover tightly with foil and roast with the rind for 30 minutes.

3 Turn down the oven setting to 190°C/375°F/Gas 5 and cook the rind for a further 30 minutes and the roast for a further hour.

4 Remove the foil and roast the meat uncovered for 20 minutes.

5 Meanwhile, prepare the apples. In a pan, melt the butter and cook the onion gently until soft but not browned, about 10 minutes. Off the heat, add the lemon zest, breadcrumbs and rosemary. Season well. Core the apples. Cut a line through the skin all round the waist of each. Fill each apple with onion stuffing. Mix the vinegar and redcurrant jelly for the glaze.

6 Remove the pork from the oven. Turn the oven setting to 200°C/400°F/Gas 6. Stand the apples around the pork, brush the pork with a little glaze and drizzle a little over the apples. Return to the oven and roast with the rind also in the oven, uncovered, for a further 20-25 minutes. Baste the pork twice with the juices and brush once with any remaining glaze. Test the pork by piercing in the centre with a skewer. The juices should run clear, not pink. If in doubt, remove the apples, keep warm, cover the pork with foil and cook for 10-15 minutes more.

7 Put the pork and apples on a warmed plate, cover with foil and leave in a warm place for 15 minutes. Spoon off the excess fat from the tin and put the tin on the stove over a medium-high heat. Pour in the stock. Boil vigorously for 5-6 minutes. Taste and season, adding a little more jelly and/or cider vinegar to taste. Strain into a gravy boat. Serve the pork and apples with the crackling, garnished with rosemary.

roasts with a twist

Accepting that part of the comfort to be found in a roast lies in its sheer simplicity and predictability, you can have a lot of fun playing with the basic concept, and dressing it up or down. You can marinate the meat ahead of time for more flavour, roast interesting and varied accompaniments with it or even give it a quite different feel as in the Oriental take on the beef marinated in soy sauce and sake.

pot-roasted brisket with pancetta and red wine

Serves 6-8
Preparation 30 minutes
Cooking about 2³/₄ hours, plus 10
  minutes' resting

1 boned and rolled brisket of beef, about
  1.8kg/4lb
salt and pepper
85g/3oz pancetta, chopped
2 garlic cloves, cut into thin slivers
1 tsp chopped fresh thyme, plus a few
  whole sprigs
3 tbsp olive oil
400g/14oz baby onions or shallots
450g/1lb small (not baby) young carrots
2–3 celery stalks, finely chopped
1 bottle of fruity red wine
2–3 bay leaves
2 tbsp tomato purée
1 tsp light muscovado sugar

1 Wipe the meat dry and season. Mix half the pancetta, the garlic, chopped thyme and ¹/₂ teaspoon salt. Make deep incisions in the beef, then push the mixture into these with the handle of a small spoon.
2 Preheat the oven to 180°C/350F°/ Gas 4. Heat the oil in a deep flameproof casserole and brown the beef on all sides. Remove and set aside. Brown the onions and remove. Lower the heat. Cook the rest of the pancetta, 2 of the carrots and the celery gently for 6 minutes.
3 Return the beef to the pan. Add the wine, thyme sprigs, bay leaves, tomato purée and sugar. Season and bring to a simmer. Cover and roast for 1 hour 50 minutes, turning the meat once.
4 Take from the oven and add the onions and remaining carrots, finely chopped. Cover again and return to the oven for 50 minutes, until carrots and meat are tender.
5 Place the vegetables and meat on a dish, cover with foil to keep warm and leave for 10 minutes. Boil the pan juices to thicken them and season with salt and pepper. Serve with the sliced meat and the vegetables.

roasted sirloin with red onions and port gravy

Serves 6-8
Preparation 15 minutes
Cooking 1¹/₂ hours

Sirloin is an expensive cut of beef, but rewards you with tender succulent slices.

about 1.3kg/3lb boneless sirloin joint
salt and pepper
4 red onions
2 tbsp olive oil
4 tbsp chopped fresh parsley
1 tbsp chopped fresh thyme or 1 tsp dried
1 tbsp chopped fresh rosemary or 1 tsp dried
2 tbsp horseradish sauce

for the gravy
1 tbsp plain flour
150ml/¹/₄ pint port
300ml/¹/₂ pint stock or cooking water
  from accompanying vegetables
1 tsp Worcestershire sauce

1 Preheat the oven to 180°C/350°F/ Gas 4. Wipe the meat and season all over with salt and pepper. Quarter the onions through the root, but keeping the root itself intact to hold them together. Peel the onion quarters.

2 Heat the oil in the roasting tin and add the onions, turning them until they are glistening. Put the beef in the tin and surround with the onions. Mix the herbs together.

3 Roast the meat for 1¼–1½ hours for medium. Cooking time depends on the shape of your joint (if it is plump, it will take longer than a long thin piece). Halfway through the cooking time, spread the horseradish over the fat of the meat, sprinkle three-quarters of the herbs over the meat and the rest over the onions.

4 Transfer the cooked meat and onions to a warm serving platter. Cover with foil and keep warm.

5 Make the gravy: reheat the pan juices in the tin, stir in the flour and cook for 1 minute. Stir in the port, followed by the stock. Bring to the boil, stirring until thickened. Add the Worcestershire sauce and simmer for 5 minutes. Taste and season.

soy and saké-marinated striploin of beef

Striploin is simply butcher's parlance for bone-free sirloin: ask for the middle-to-rump part of the sirloin.

Serves 6
Preparation 15-25 minutes, plus
  6-24 hours' marinating
Cooking 30 minutes

about 1.7kg/3lb 12oz Scottish striploin
  (boned sirloin)
4 tbsp saké or very dry sherry
4 tbsp soy sauce or tamari
4 tbsp rice wine vinegar
1 tbsp golden caster sugar
2–3 garlic cloves, peeled, crushed and
  finely chopped
1 'thumb' of root ginger, peeled and grated
1 tbsp groundnut or vegetable oil

1 Remove the skin and back fat from the striploin, then trim off any other tissue or fat so the joint looks as clean as a fillet steak with no more than 1cm/½in of fat left. Put the beef into a deepish, non-reactive, fairly tight-fitting dish.

2 Whisk all the other ingredients, except for the oil, with 4 tablespoons cold water. Pour this over the beef, turning it to coat well. Cover and chill for 6–24 hours, turning the beef every few hours, or when you remember.

3 When you are ready to cook the beef, preheat the oven to 220°C/ 425°F/Gas 7. Take the joint out of the marinade and pat it as dry as you can with kitchen paper.

4 Put a large frying pan over a high flame and, while it's heating up, smear the oil over the beef, using the palms of your hands. Put the beef into the searingly hot pan and brown it very quickly on all sides (including the ends), using a pair of stout tongs to turn it.

5 Transfer the meat to a metal rack set in a roasting tin. Put the tin on the middle shelf of the oven and roast the beef for 30 minutes, if you like your meat medium-rare in the middle. Cook it for another 10-15 minutes if you prefer it less pink, but this is not a recipe that lends itself to well-done beef - without any protective fat, the meat will be very dry.

6 Leave the beef to rest in a warm place for 10-15 minutes, then transfer the joint to a carving board or platter, and slice it fairly thinly.

mint and lemon roast lamb

Serves 6-8
**Preparation 25 minutes, plus at least
  1 hour's marinating**
Cooking 1 hour −1 hour 40 minutes

1 leg of lamb, about 1.8–2kg/4–4¹/₂lb
2 lemons, preferably unwaxed
3 garlic cloves
4 tbsp chopped mint
4 tbsp olive oil
salt and pepper

for the gravy
2 rounded tsp plain flour
300ml/¹/₂ pint vegetable stock
150ml/¹/₄ pint red wine
2 tsp mustard (English or Dijon)
1 tbsp redcurrant or cranberry jelly

1 Wipe the lamb with kitchen paper, then make about 10 large, deep cuts in the flesh with a sharp knife. Grate the zest of 1¹/₂ lemons, squeeze their juice and finely chop the garlic. Mix the lemon zest and juice, garlic, mint, oil, salt and pepper in a small bowl. Put the lamb in a large food bag (a pedal bin liner is ideal). Pour the mint and lemon mixture into the bag, then rub it into the lamb through the bag (this saves your hands getting messy). Loosely fold the end of the bag over and put the lamb in the fridge for at least an hour, or overnight if more convenient.

2 Preheat the oven to 190°C/375°F/Gas 5. Put the lamb in a roasting tin and pour over any remaining marinade. Add 3 tablespoons of water to the roasting tin to help stop the juices from burning. Thinly slice the remaining half lemon, then cut each slice in half. Fold the slices in half again and firmly push into the cuts in the meat. Roast the lamb for 1-1¹/₄ hours for moist pink meat. If you prefer it more well done, roast for a further 15-25 minutes. Transfer the lamb to a warm serving platter and cover with foil. Leave to rest for 15 minutes while you make the gravy.

3 Set the roasting tin over a medium heat. Spoon off excess fat, then stir the flour into the pan juices to form a paste. Gradually stir in the stock, then the wine, stirring all the time until thick and smooth. Stir in the mustard and jelly, and simmer for 5 minutes. Adjust the seasoning if necessary. Serve with the carved lamb.

spiced lamb casserole

Preparation about 15 minutes
Cooking about 30 minutes

550g/1¼lb diced lamb
salt and pepper
1 tbsp plain flour
2 tbsp olive oil
2 onions, chopped
3 large carrots, cut into chunks
2 garlic cloves, finely chopped
*600ml/1 pint lamb, chicken or vegetable
  stock*
1 tbsp cranberry sauce
2 tsp tomato paste
12 pitted ready-to-eat dates
3 tbsp chopped fresh parsley

*This casserole is very nice served with some plain low-fat yoghurt into which you
have stirred some chopped fresh mint and lemon juice, plus salt and pepper to taste.*

1 Put the lamb into a plastic bag with the seasoned flour and shake vigorously until
the lamb is evenly coated. Remove the lamb and shake off any excess flour.

2 Heat the oil in a large saucepan or flameproof casserole. Add the lamb, onion and
carrots, and fry over a moderate-to-high heat for 8-10 minutes, stirring often, until
nicely golden all over. Add the garlic and cook for 1 minute.

3 Add the stock and bring to the boil. Reduce the heat and simmer gently,
covered, for 20 minutes until thickened slightly. Stir in the cranberry sauce, tomato
paste, dates and parsley, together with some salt and pepper to taste. Heat through
gently and serve with rice or couscous.

Serves 6
Preparation 55 minutes
Cooking 50 minutes

about 2 tbsp olive oil, plus extra for
  greasing and frying
2 tsp ground cumin
2 tsp ground cinnamon
a little freshly grated nutmeg
2 large aubergines, thinly sliced
225g/8oz chestnut mushrooms, sliced
450g/1lb lamb leg fillet, trimmed of as
  much fat as possible
100g/4oz dried apricots, chopped
85g/3oz seedless raisins
double quantity of tomato sauce (see page 100)
2 eggs, lightly beaten
350ml/12fl oz Greek-style yoghurt

lamb and apricot moussaka

1 Preheat the grill and lightly oil a large ovenproof casserole. Mix the olive oil and spices together and brush over the aubergine slices. Grill for 4-5 minutes on each side, until crisp and golden. Set aside. Heat a little oil in a frying pan and fry the mushrooms for 3-4 minutes until golden.

2 Heat a non-stick frying pan until very hot, then fry the lamb fillets for 3-5 minutes on each side until seared and well browned. Leave to cool until they can be handled, then cut across the grain into chunky slices. Where necessary, cut the slices into bite-sized pieces.

3 Preheat the oven to 180°C/350°F/Gas 4. Layer half the aubergines in the bottom of the casserole. Mix the dried fruit into the tomato sauce. Spoon a third over the aubergines, top with the mushrooms, then another layer of sauce, the lamb, another layer of sauce and a top layer of aubergines.

4 Mix the eggs into the yogurt and season with black pepper. Pour over the top of the dish and bake for about 45 minutes, then finish off by grilling for 5 minutes, until golden.

beef en daube

This recipe has got everything – lots of Mediterranean flavour, tender meat, crispy bacon, wholesome veggies and plenty of gravy.

1 Well ahead, ideally the day before, make the marinade: heat the olive oil in a small pan, add the onion, celery and carrot, and cook for about 2 minutes until softened. Add the garlic, red wine, peppercorns, herb sprigs, bay leaf and parsley. Bring to the boil, then simmer for 15-20 minutes. Allow to cool, then pour over the beef in a non-metallic dish. Leave to marinate for at least 12 hours, preferably overnight, turning the meat once or twice.

2 Preheat the oven to 160°C/325°F/Gas 3. In a casserole dish, fry the bacon until crisp, then remove from the pan. Add the drained beef and brown it on all sides. Return the bacon to the pan, then add the carrots, thyme, rosemary, bay leaf and garlic. Strain the marinade into the casserole, cover with a circle of greaseproof paper and a lid and cook for 2 hours.

3 Add the olives and tomatoes and cook for 30 minutes more.

4 Cut the beef into thick slices and serve with the sauce and mashed potatoes.

Serves 4-6

Preparation 20 minutes, plus 12 hours' marinating

Cooking about 3 hours

1.3kg/3lb topside or silverside of beef
12 unsmoked streaky bacon rashers
2 carrots, thickly sliced
2 fresh thyme sprigs
1 small rosemary sprig
1 bay leaf
3 garlic cloves, crushed
175g/6oz pitted black olives
230g/8oz can of tomatoes

for the marinade
3 tbsp olive oil
1 onion, sliced
1 small celery stalk, sliced
1 carrot, sliced
2 garlic cloves, thinly sliced
150ml/¼ pint red wine
6 black peppercorns
2 fresh thyme sprigs
1 small rosemary sprig
1 bay leaf
2 parsley stalks

lamb and red pepper stew

Preparation 10-15 minutes
Cooking 50-55 minutes

600g/1¼lb boneless lamb fillet, cut into
  small chunks
25g/1oz plain flour
salt and pepper
3 tbsp olive oil
3 garlic cloves, crushed
150ml/¼ pint dry white wine
3 small red peppers or 2 large ones,
  halved, deseeded and cut into
  5cm/2in pieces
150ml/¼ pint tomato passata
225ml/8fl oz lamb, chicken or vegetable
  stock
3 bay leaves
100g/4oz ready-to-eat dried apricots

1 Put the cubes of lamb into a plastic bag with the seasoned flour and shake vigorously until the lamb is evenly coated. Heat the oil in a large saucepan or flameproof casserole dish. Add half the lamb and fry, turning now and then, until nicely browned all over. Lift on to a plate and repeat with the remaining lamb.

2 Return the first batch of meat to the pan with the garlic and cook for 1 minute. Add any flour left in the bag and cook for another minute.

3 Pour the wine into the pan and, scraping the residue, cook over a high heat until it has reduced by about one-third.

4 Stir in the red peppers, passata, stock, bay leaves and a little seasoning. Cover and simmer for 30 minutes or until the lamb is tender. Add the apricots and simmer for a further 5 minutes. Serve with rice, mash or jacket potatoes.

Variation
Use chicken instead of lamb and reduce the cooking time to 20 minutes.

chicken casserole with rosemary dumplings

Preparation 15 minutes
Cooking 1 hour 20 minutes

4–6 smoked streaky bacon rashers
4–6 boneless skinless chicken thighs
1 sweet potato (about 250g/9oz)
2 tbsp oil
2 carrots, roughly chopped
8 pickling onions, peeled
2 tbsp plain flour
1 tsp tomato paste
300ml/½ pint dry white wine
1 good-quality chicken stock cube
2 tbsp chopped fresh coriander

for the rosemary dumplings
225g/8oz self-raising flour
100g/4oz shredded suet
2 tbsp chopped fresh rosemary
1 egg, beaten

1 Preheat the oven to 180°C/350°F/Gas 4. Wrap a bacon rasher around each chicken thigh and secure with a cocktail stick. Season. Peel the sweet potato and cut into 2cm/¾in cubes. Heat the oil in a large frying pan and fry the sweet potato and carrots for 8-10 minutes until golden. Remove with a slotted spoon and drain. Add the onions to the pan and cook for about 5 minutes until browned. Remove the onions and cook the chicken until browned all over. Remove from the heat.

2 Transfer the vegetables to an ovenproof casserole and stir in the flour. Add 600ml/ 1 pint boiling water, then stir in the tomato paste, wine and stock cube. Season. Top with the chicken and bring to the boil. Cover and bake for 20 minutes.

3 Make the dumpling by mixing all the ingredients with just enough water (about 5-6 tablespoons) to form a smooth dough. Knead well. Roll into 8 balls and add to the casserole. Bake, uncovered, for 35 minutes until they are browned and crisp.

4 To serve, remove the sticks from the chicken and sprinkle with coriander.

butternut squash and spiced lamb stew

Preparation 30-40 minutes
Cooking 1 hour 25 minutes

3 tbsp olive oil
900g/2lb lamb neck fillet, trimmed and
*   cut into bite-sized pieces*
1 onion, roughly chopped
2 garlic cloves, crushed
2.5cm/1in piece of root ginger, grated
1 tbsp tomato purée
1 tbsp harissa paste
25g/1oz plain flour
1.2 litres/2 pints lamb or vegetable stock
1.3kg/3lb butternut squash
4 tomatoes, skinned, deseeded and chopped
400g/14oz can of chickpeas, drained and
*   rinsed*
225g/8oz baby spinach
2 tbsp lemon juice
salt and pepper

Harissa is a fiery chilli paste from North Africa that is widely available in supermarkets in tubes or in jars. Curry paste is a good alternative if you can't find it, though the taste will be different.

1 Heat the oil in a large saucepan, add the lamb and cook over a high heat for 4-5 minutes until browned all over, stirring occasionally. Add the onion, garlic and ginger and cook for 3-4 minutes until softened. Stir in the tomato purée, harissa and flour, and cook over a medium heat for 1-2 minutes. Pour in the stock, bring to the boil, cover and simmer for 45 minutes.

2 Cut the squash in half and scoop out the seeds. Peel and cut the flesh into bite-sized chunks.

3 Add the tomatoes, squash and chickpeas to the lamb mixture and cook for 30 minutes, stirring occasionally.

4 Stir in the spinach and lemon juice and cook for a further 1-2 minutes. Season and serve with crusty bread.

quick seafood paella

Preparation 10-15 minutes
Cooking about 25 minutes

1 tbsp sunflower oil
1 onion, finely chopped
1 red pepper, deseeded and sliced
2 garlic cloves, finely chopped
230g/8oz can of chopped tomatoes
1 tsp ground turmeric
300g/10oz long-grain rice
1.3 litres/2¼ pints vegetable stock
450g/1lb frozen mixed seafood (prawns, mussels and squid rings), defrosted
175g/6oz green beans, halved
handful of chopped fresh parsley
salt and pepper
1 lemon, cut into wedges

1 Heat the oil in a large frying pan and cook the onion and pepper for 5 minutes until softened but not brown. Stir in the garlic, tomatoes and turmeric, and cook for 1 minute more, stirring occasionally.

2 Tip in the rice and cook for 1 minute, stirring to coat the grains. Pour in the stock, stir well and bring to the boil, then simmer uncovered for 8 minutes, stirring occasionally, until the rice is almost cooked and most of the stock has been absorbed.

3 Add the seafood and beans, and cook for 3-4 minutes more.

4 Stir in the parsley and season to taste. Serve the paella straight from the pan, with lemon wedges.

Spanish-style baked fish

Serves 6
Preparation 20-30 minutes
Cooking about 1 hour

1kg/2¼lb waxy new potatoes, such as
   Charlotte, thinly sliced
4 garlic cloves, thinly sliced
2 large red onions, cut into wedges
2 red peppers, deseeded and cut into
   chunks
2 yellow peppers, deseeded and cut into
   chunks
5 tbsp extra-virgin olive oil
150g/5oz black olives
6 bay leaves
6 thick-cut haddock or cod fillets, each
   about 175g/6oz
juice of 1 small lemon
150g/5oz pot of fresh pesto sauce
salt and pepper
lemon wedges and crisp green salad, to
   serve

This treatment would suit lots of different fish, from firm-fleshed, meaty ones like swordfish to the oily ones, like salmon, sardines and mackerel.

1 Preheat the oven to 200°C/400°F/Gas 6. Pat the sliced potatoes dry with kitchen paper and toss with the garlic, onions, peppers and 4 tablespoons of the oil in a large shallow roasting tin or ovenproof dish – make sure it's large and shallow so the vegetables have room to roast. Roast for 45 minutes until the vegetables begin to soften and turn golden.

2 Scatter the black olives and bay leaves over the vegetables. Then sit the fish on top in one layer, skin side down. Mix the remaining oil, lemon juice and pesto together, and spoon over the fish fillets. Season with a little salt and plenty of freshly ground black pepper. Roast in the oven for 15 minutes.

3 Serve immediately with wedges of lemon and a crisp green salad.

herby cod bake

Preparation 10 minutes
Cooking about 5 minutes

125ml/4fl oz natural low-fat yoghurt
4 tbsp sun-dried tomato pesto
4 tbsp chopped fresh parsley or dill
salt and pepper
4 cod or haddock fillets, each about
   175g/6oz, skinned

This dish is as fast and easy as it is tasty and satisfying. If you can't find sun-dried tomato pesto, mix equal parts ordinary pesto and sun-dried tomato paste.

1 Preheat a hot grill. Mix together the yoghurt, pesto and half the herbs. Season and pour over the fish fillets in a shallow ovenproof or microwavable dish to cover them completely.

2 Grill for 4–5 minutes, without turning, until the fish fillets are cooked through to the middle. Alternatively, cover the dish and microwave on High for 3 minutes.

3 Sprinkle with the remaining herbs and serve with a salad and crusty or garlic bread.

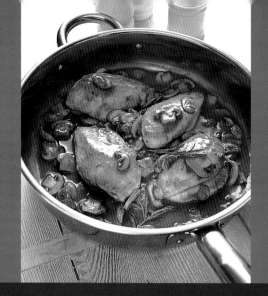

guilt-free indulgences

Yes, it is possible to wallow in comfort food and yet still not drown in fat and/or calories. Fish and lean chicken breast are the best candidates for this sort of dish, with the surprise addition of pork fillet, which is nowadays incredibly low in fat. Bulk out with lots of vegetables and/or rice and cook with the minimum of added fat, and you can enjoy the most hearty feast without blowing your diet.

glazed chicken with potato and celeriac mash

Preparation 15 minutes
Cooking 35 minutes

4 boneless, skinless chicken breasts, each about 150g/5oz
1 tbsp olive oil
100g/4oz chestnut mushrooms, sliced
1 tbsp plain flour
600ml/1 pint chicken stock
1 tbsp tomato purée
2 fresh rosemary sprigs
2 tbsp redcurrant jelly

for the mash
3 large potatoes, or about 700g/1lb 9oz, peeled and chopped
200g/7oz celeriac, peeled and chopped
salt and pepper
3 tbsp semi-skimmed milk
8 spring onions, trimmed and chopped

1 Heat a large pan, brush the chicken breasts with oil and brown them in the pan for about 4 minutes on each side. Remove from the pan and set aside.
2 Add the mushrooms to the pan and cook until brown. Add the flour and cook for a few minutes, stirring, until it browns. Pour in the stock, stirring. Bring to the boil, stir in the tomato purée and rosemary, and put the chicken back in. Cover the pan and cook over a gentle heat for 15-20 minutes until just tender.
3 While the chicken cooks, make the mash: simmer the potatoes and celeriac in a large pan of boiling salted water for about 12 minutes until tender. Drain and return to the pan, covered, to dry them out. In a small pan, gently heat the milk, add the spring onions and cook until softened. Mash the potatoes and celeriac with the milk and spring onions. Season to taste.
4 Stir the redcurrant jelly into the chicken. Turn the heat up to reduce the sauce so it coats the chicken. Serve with the mash.

fish o'leekie

Preparation 10 minutes
Cooking 20 minutes

1 leek, thinly sliced
100g/4oz lean smoked back bacon
500ml/18fl oz hot fish or vegetable stock
300g/10oz American easy-cook rice
500g/1lb 2oz cod or haddock fillets, skinned and cut into largish chunks
3 tbsp chopped fresh parsley
grated zest and juice of 1 lemon

1 Put the leeks and bacon in a medium microwavable dish with 4 tablespoons of the stock. Cover with cling film, pierce the film with the tip of a knife and microwave on High for 5 minutes.
2 Stir the rice and remaining stock into the leek and bacon, and continue to cook, uncovered, in the microwave for a further 5 minutes. Gently stir in the fish chunks, cover with cling film, pierce with a knife and cook for a further 10 minutes, until the fish and rice are cooked.

3 Stir in the parsley, lemon zest and juice. Leave to stand for for 2–3 minutes and serve straight from the dish.

Variation

If you haven't got a microwave cooker, first poach the fish gently in the stock until just flaking. Carefully remove with a slotted spoon and then boil the rice in the stock according to packet instructions. While that is cooking, dry-fry the bacon until cooked, remove from the pan and stir-fry the leek in the bacon fat. When the rice is cooked and drained, mix everything together with the parsley, lemon zest and juice.

pork fillet with roast vegetables

Preparation 25-35 minutes
Cooking 55-70 minutes

4 medium parsnips, quartered lengthwise
1 butternut squash (about 650g/1½lb), peeled, deseeded and cut into chunks
2 red onions, each cut into 8 wedges
1 tbsp olive oil
salt and pepper

grated zest of 1 lemon
2 tsp dried mixed Italian herbs
500g/1lb 2oz lean pork tenderloin, in 1 or 2 pieces
1 medium cooking apple
400ml/14fl oz chicken stock

1 Preheat the oven to 200°C/400°F/ Gas 6. Put the vegetables into a roasting pan. Drizzle with olive oil, season and toss together.
2 On a plate, mix the lemon zest and herbs. Roll the pork in the mix and place on the vegetables. Roast for 40-50 minutes.
3 Peel the apple, core and cut into chunks. Put in the roasting tin, add the stock and cook for 15-20 minutes.
4 Serve the pork cut into slices, with the vegetables and pan juices spooned over.

Variation

You can replace the pork with skinless chicken breasts and roast this for just the last 30 minutes of cooking time.

Spreading
cheer

ALTHOUGH THE COMFORT CONCEPT IS MOST USUALLY

LINKED WITH HEARTH, HOME AND FAMILY, SOME

DISHES COMBINE IT WITH SUFFICIENT WOW FACTOR TO

MAKE THEM EXCELLENT CANDIDATES FOR

ENTERTAINING.

wild mushroom tart with goats' cheese

Serves 6
Preparation 30-40 minutes
Cooking 1 hour

200ml/7fl oz milk
150ml/¹/4 pint double cream
1 garlic clove, crushed
350g/12oz floury potatoes such as King
Edward's, peeled and thinly sliced
50g/2oz butter
350g/12oz mixed wild mushrooms, such
as chanterelles and ceps, roughly sliced
salt and pepper
250g/9oz frozen puff pastry, defrosted
flour, for dusting
100g/4oz goats' cheese, diced

1 Pour the milk and cream into a large heavy saucepan and add the crushed garlic. Bring to the boil and tip in the potatoes. Bring back to the boil and simmer very gently for 10-15 minutes, stirring from time to time, until the potatoes are tender.

2 Meanwhile, preheat the oven to 200°C/400°F/Gas 6 and put a baking sheet to heat at the same time. Melt the butter in a large frying pan. When it begins to foam and sizzle, add the sliced mushrooms and cook over a high heat for about 10 minutes or until all the pan juices have evaporated. Remove the mushrooms from the heat and season. When the potatoes are tender, remove from the heat and season well.

3 Roll out the pastry on a lightly floured surface and use to line a 23cm/9in loose-bottomed quiche tin. Fill with the potato mixture, spreading it out evenly, then spread the mushrooms on top and scatter with the cheese. Slide the tart on to the hot baking sheet and bake for 20-25 minutes or until the pastry is crisp and golden brown. Serve hot with a leafy green salad.

venison and mushroom pie

Serves 6
Preparation 20 minutes, plus 1-2
days' marinating
Cooking 2³/4 hours

500g/1lb 2oz boneless venison from the
haunch (see introduction), trimmed and
cut into 4cm/1¹/2in pieces
500g/1lb 2oz chuck steak, trimmed and
cut into 4cm/1¹/2in pieces
200ml/7fl oz tawny port
4 shallots, finely chopped
1 tbsp pickled walnuts, finely chopped
25g/1oz plain flour
salt and pepper
700ml/1¹/4 pint beef stock
500g/1lb 2oz portobello or large flat
mushrooms, cut into wedges
500g/1lb 2oz puff pastry
1 egg, beaten, to glaze

For a pie, stewing venison is a false economy as it tends to be tough and sinewy. Haunch does well and is not too expensive – ask the butcher to trim it and remove the bone. Pickled walnuts in jars are available from good delicatessens.

1 Put the venison and steak pieces in a heavy plastic food bag and add the port. Seal and leave to marinate in a bowl in the fridge for at least a day or two.

2 Preheat the oven to 180°C/350°F/Gas 4. In a large bowl, mix the shallots, walnuts and flour with a teaspoon each of salt and pepper. With a slotted spoon, lift the meat from the port, reserving that, and stir it into the flour, coating thoroughly. Transfer to a large ovenproof casserole. Stir together the reserved port and stock, and stir into the casserole along with the mushrooms. Bring to the boil over a medium heat. Cover and put in the oven for 2 hours, until the meat is tender. Remove the lid, bring to the boil over high heat and simmer for 15-20 minutes to thicken. Season. Put in a 1.75 litre/3 pint pie dish and leave to cool.

3 Roll the pastry out to an oval 2.5cm/1in larger than the dish. Trim and cut a strip the width of the dish rim from the edge. Wet the rim and press the strip on it. Brush the strip with the egg glaze. Lift the dough on to the pie dish. Press firmly to seal it to the strip. Trim and brush the top with the egg glaze. Make 2 small slits in the centre for steam. Roll out trimmings and cut out flowers or leaves to decorate. Brush with the egg mixed with ¹/2 teaspoon salt. Chill for at least 15 minutes. Turn oven to 220°C/425°F/Gas 7 and bake for 30 minutes or until puffed and golden.

salmon en croûte

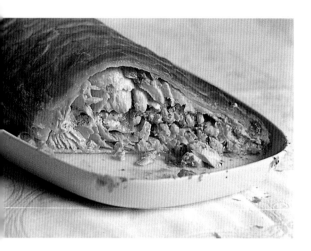

Two salmon fillets are sandwiched with chopped summer herbs blended with soft cheese, prawns and tomatoes, then sealed in puff pastry and baked to a golden crust. If you're choosing a whole salmon from the fish counter, look for a glossy skin and bright eyes that are not sunken. Ask the fishmonger to fillet the salmon into two pieces and remove the skin. You'll need a 2–2.25kg/4½–5lb salmon before skinning and boning.

Serves 6-8

Preparation 30 minutes, plus 30 minutes' chilling

Cooking 35 minutes

1 salmon, weighing 1.3–1.6kg/3–3½lb, skinned and filleted (see introduction)
salt and pepper
good bunch of fresh parsley
3–4 fresh tarragon sprigs
handful of fresh chives
225g/8oz peeled cooked prawns
3 ripe tomatoes, skinned, deseeded and chopped (about 250g/9oz)
200g/7oz full- or half-fat soft cheese
1 tbsp lemon juice
500g/1lb 2oz puff pastry, defrosted if frozen
beaten egg, to glaze

1 Season the salmon all over with salt and pepper.

2 Chop the parsley. Strip the tarragon leaves from the stems and chop the leaves. Mix the two herbs in a bowl, then snip in the chives. Add the prawns and mix together.

3 Put the tomatoes in a bowl and pour over boiling water from a kettle to cover. Leave for 2 minutes, then drain and slip off the skins. Halve the tomatoes, then squeeze out and discard the seeds. Chop the flesh and add to the herbs along with the soft cheese, lemon juice, salt and pepper. Stir well to mix and adjust the seasoning if necessary.

4 Lay a salmon fillet, skinned-side down, on a board and spread with the prawn and cheese filling. Put the second fillet on top, skinned-side up.

5 Roll out half the pastry so it's about 2.5cm/1in larger all round than the fish. Lay the pastry on a dampened baking sheet and put the salmon on top. Brush the edges of the pastry with beaten egg. Roll out the remaining pastry so it's a little larger than the first piece. Lift it carefully over the salmon and press the edges all round to seal. Trim off the excess pastry using a sharp knife. Pinch the edges of the pastry between your fingers and thumb all the way round to seal it. Starting at the head end, use a teaspoon to mark the pastry with semicircles, to represent scales. Chill for at least 30 minutes, or overnight if more convenient.

6 Preheat the oven to 220°C/425°F/Gas 7. Brush the pastry liberally with beaten egg and bake for 15 minutes, then brush again with egg. Reduce the oven setting to 180°C/350°F/Gas 4, then bake for a further 20 minutes until the pastry is crisp and golden brown.

7 Salmon en croûte is great served warm or at room temperature, cut into thickish slices, with some buttered new potatoes or a potato salad. Serve a green salad on the side – use peppery leaves, such as watercress, rocket or lamb's lettuce, dressed lightly with lemon juice and a light olive oil (1 part lemon juice to 3 parts olive oil, plus a little mustard, salt and pepper).

salmon and caper baklava pie

Serves 4-6
Preparation 25 minutes
Cooking 20 minutes

450g/1lb salmon fillet, skinned and cut
* into dice*
1 large shallot, finely chopped
2 tbsp baby capers, drained and rinsed
1 red chilli, deseeded and finely chopped
100g/4oz Greek-style yoghurt
1 egg, beaten
salt and pepper
140g/5oz filo pastry, cut into eight 23x
* 30cm/9x12in pieces*
1 tbsp light olive oil
3 tbsp dried breadcrumbs
1 tbsp sesame seeds
200g/7oz extra-fine green beans

for the dressing
2 tbsp light olive oil
1/2 tsp clear honey
juice of 1 medium orange
2 tbsp finely chopped fresh mint

This modern, stylish low-fat fish pie is perfect for summer entertaining.

1 Preheat the oven to 180°C/350°F/Gas 4. In a large bowl, combine the salmon, shallot, capers, chilli, yogurt and egg. Season to taste.

2 Brush 4 sheets of filo with a little oil. Layer the sheets up on a large non-stick baking sheet and sprinkle over the dried breadcrumbs. Spoon over the salmon mixture, top with another filo sheet and lightly press. Brush with oil, top with the remaining filo, brushing each sheet with oil. Score a criss-cross pattern on top and sprinkle with sesame seeds. Bake for 20 minutes.

3 Make the dressing by mixing all the ingredients together.

4 About 5 minutes before serving, cook the beans in boiling salted water to cover until just tender. Drain and toss with 1-2 tablespoons of the dressing.

5 Cut the pie into diamonds, pour over the remaining dressing and serve with the green beans.

potting comfort

As they are basically very luxurious sandwich spreads, pâtés, terrines and potted meats and fish make the most comforting of dinner party starters. The whole process of scooping up the scrumminess and spreading it thickly on toast or chunks of crusty bread takes us back to our childhood – and then there's the exquisite buttery mouth-feel and full, rich flavour.

potted salmon

This is an ideal dish to make with leftover fish from a whole baked or poached salmon.

Serves 8
Preparation 10 minutes, plus 30 minutes' chilling
Cooking 10 minutes (for the salmon)

400g/14oz cooked skinned salmon, in chunks
100g/4oz unsalted butter, well softened
5–6 canned anchovy fillets, drained and snipped
¼ tsp ground mace
a good pinch of cayenne pepper
oatcakes or hot toast, to serve
chopped parsley and coarse black pepper, for sprinkling

1 Put the salmon, butter, anchovy fillets, mace and cayenne in a bowl and pound with a wooden spoon until combined but still chunky. You can use a food processor, but be sure to use the pulse button: you want a rough texture. Season to taste with salt and pepper, bearing in mind that the anchovies are very salty.
2 Pile into small individual ramekins, cover and refrigerate for at least 30 minutes, or until ready to serve, sprinkled with parsley and black pepper. You can prepare up to 2 days in advance and chill.

old-fashioned and buttery potted shrimps

Preparation 45 minutes
Cooking about 1 minute, plus cooling

400g/14oz brown shrimps in their shells
200g/8oz unsalted butter
¼ tsp cayenne pepper
½ tsp ground mace
1 small garlic clove, crushed
1 heaped tbsp chopped fresh parsley

8 slices of white bread

1 Peel the shrimps - this will take about 30 minutes (less, if you get a friend to help).
2 Melt the butter over a low heat until it foams, then pour it into a bowl. Leave to cool slightly for about 10 minutes until the butter separates. Using a spoon, carefully skim off the milk solids from the surface and discard. The clear oil that is left is clarified butter.
3 Heat the shrimps in a frying pan with 2 tablespoons of clarified butter. Stir in the cayenne, mace and garlic. Turn up the heat and stir-fry for about 30 seconds until the butter is very hot, then remove the pan from the heat and add the parsley.
4 Spoon into 4 small ramekins or dishes about 7.5cm/3in in diameter. Divide the shrimps equally between the dishes, pressing them down with the back of a spoon. Pour the rest of the clarified butter over the shrimps to cover, then put in a cool place to set. (You can put them in the fridge, but

remove them about an hour before serving, to allow the butter to soften and reach room temperature.)

5 When they have set, serve with warm melba toast. To make this, lightly toast the slices of white bread. Cut off the crusts, then slice the bread across its depth, so you have 16 ultra-thin slices. Put the toast, cut-side up, under a medium-to-hot grill until fully toasted and the edges curl. Be careful, as it burns easily.

pork and duck terrine

Serves 8-10
Preparation 45 minutes
Cooking 2¼ hours

2 duck breasts, about 350g/12oz in total
225g/8oz rindless streaky bacon
450g/1lb pork shoulder
450g/1lb minced pork
1 garlic clove, finely chopped
5 juniper berries
1 tsp mixed peppercorns
3 tbsp brandy
1½–2 tsp salt, depending on taste
2 tsp fresh thyme leaves or 1 tsp dried

1 Preheat the oven to 160°C/325°F/ Gas 3. Using a small sharp knife, remove the skin from the duck. Set the duck meat aside for later. Put the duck skin in an ovenproof dish and bake for 20 minutes to melt the fat.

2 Meanwhile, using scissors, remove a thin strip of fat from each bacon rasher and set aside for the lattice top. Chop the trimmed bacon rashers, the duck meat and pork shoulder into small pieces about the size of peas and put them in a bowl with the minced pork. Mix well (hands are probably best for this job as you can squeeze the mixture with your fingers to ensure everything is well blended, but if you can't bear to do this, use a large fork).

3 Remove the duck fat from the oven and discard the small pieces of unmelted skin. Stir the garlic into the melted fat and set aside.

4 Using a pestle and mortar, grind the juniper berries and peppercorns fairly coarsely. Add to the meat mixture, along with the brandy, garlic and duck fat, salt and thyme. Mix thoroughly.

5 Press the mixture into a wide and shallow 850ml/1½ pint ovenproof dish, then smooth the top, mounding it up in the centre. Arrange the reserved bacon fat in a lattice pattern over the top, tucking in the ends with the back of a knife. Cover with foil and put in a deep roasting tin. Pour boiling water into the tin to come halfway up the sides of the dish.

6 Put in the oven for 2 hours, then remove the foil and cook for a further 15 minutes to brown the top. Leave to cool, cover with fresh foil and chill.

7 Serve with crusty baguette, radishes and cornichons as a starter. For lunch, also serve a green or mixed salad and some raw vegetable sticks.

Tips

• Cutting the meat into small pieces by hand takes time, but a food processor would reduce the meat to a paste and you'd lose that great chunky texture. After the meat preparation, you'll sail through the rest of the recipe easily and your efforts will be amply rewarded with a wonderfully coarse-textured terrine.

• To store the terrine: when cool, cover it in fresh foil. It will keep in the fridge for up to 4 days. For the best flavour, let it come back to room temperature before serving. The terrine can also be frozen, whole or in slices, for up to 3 months. Wrap closely in freezer film, then overwrap in foil, pressing it over the surface of the terrine to exclude as much air as possible.

Serves 2
Preparation 25–35 minutes
Cooking 40 minutes

2 tbsp olive oil, plus extra for sprinkling
knob of butter
2 large onions, thinly sliced
1 tsp light muscovado sugar
6 medium-sized new potatoes
salt and pepper
250g/9oz ready-made puff pastry,
*   defrosted if frozen*
225g/8oz cherry tomatoes on the vine
100g/4oz Camembert cheese, cut into
*   slices*
6 anchovy fillets
6 unpitted black olives
1 tbsp pesto
a few basil leaves, roughly torn

for the rocket and green bean salad
50g/2oz rocket leaves, preferably wild
100g/4oz green beans, lightly steamed
a little olive oil
good squeeze of lemon juice

Mediterranean salad tarts

These tarts are packed full of fresh flavours and colours. They're really enjoyable to make.

1 Heat 1 tablespoon of oil with the butter. Add the onions and cook over a medium-low heat, stirring often, for 15–20 minutes until soft and golden brown. Stir in the sugar and cook for a further 3–4 minutes. Remove from heat.

2 Cook the potatoes in boiling salted water for about 10 minutes until just tender. Slice when cool. Preheat the oven to 220°C/425°F/Gas 7.

3 Cut the pastry in half and shape into 2 rough rounds. Roll them out on a lightly floured surface to give two 18cm/7in rounds, then put on to a baking sheet. Divide the onions between the pastry rounds, spreading them almost to cover. Reserve 2 sprigs of vine tomatoes with about 3 or 4 on each stem, and slice the rest in half. Scatter the slices of cheese over the onions, then the sliced potatoes, tomatoes and anchovy fillets. Top each tart with one of the tomato sprays, scatter the olives over and drizzle with a little extra oil. Bake for 15–20 minutes until golden.

4 Make the salad: toss the rocket and beans with a little oil and lemon juice and season.

5 When the tarts are cooked, mix the pesto with the remaining oil and drizzle this all over the tarts, then scatter the torn basil leaves on top. Serve with the salad.

cheese soufflé

Preparation 30-40 minutes
Cooking 40-45 minutes

50g/2oz butter, plus extra for greasing
4 eggs, separated
300ml/ 1/2 pint milk
1 bay leaf
50g/2oz plain flour
100g/4oz firm goats' cheese, with rind,
    finely chopped
50g/2oz freshly grated Parmesan cheese
15g/1/2oz fresh chives
salt and pepper

1 Put a heavy baking sheet on the shelf below the centre of the oven and preheat to 190°C/375°F/Gas 5. Butter the inside of a soufflé dish, greasing the rim well. Put the egg whites into a large scrupulously clean bowl and the yolks into a small bowl.

2 Pour the milk into a large pan, add the bay leaf and butter, and sprinkle in the flour. Put over medium heat, whisking vigorously, until the milk comes to the boil. Once starting to thicken, continue to whisk for 1 minute until very thick. Remove from the heat. Discard the bay leaf. Whisk in the cheeses, reserving 1 tablespoon of Parmesan. The goats' cheese will make it look lumpy. Whisk in the egg yolks, one at a time. Finely snip in the chives, then season to taste. Whisk well and set aside.

3 Whisk the whites for several minutes until just standing in soft peaks. Using a wooden spoon, stir 2 spoonfuls of the egg whites into the cheese sauce to slacken it. Using a spatula or large metal spoon, gently fold in the rest. Use a figure-of-eight motion to blend the egg whites through the sauce mixture without deflating it. Pour the mixture into the soufflé dish and sprinkle with the reserved Parmesan. Run a thumb lightly round the inside edge, making a deep groove in the mixture so the top won't stick to the rim. Place on the hot baking sheet in the oven and cook for 35-40 minutes, until risen and golden. Slowly open the oven door and shake the soufflé gently. It should wobble slightly; if it wobbles a lot, bake it for 5-10 minutes more.

lamb shanks with chickpeas and Moroccan spices

**Preparation 40 minutes, plus
overnight soaking
Cooking 3–4 hours**

175g/6oz dried chickpeas
2 tbsp olive oil
4 medium-sized lamb shanks
2 medium-sized onions, chopped
2 tsp finely chopped fresh root ginger
3 garlic cloves, finely chopped
*2 fresh green chillies, deseeded and finely
  chopped*
2 tsp ground cumin
2 tsp ground coriander
1 tsp freshly ground black pepper
1 tsp paprika
*2 large tomatoes, skinned, deseeded and
  chopped*
pinch of saffron strands
2cm/³/4in piece of cinnamon stick
450g/1lb carrots, cut into thick slices
150g/5oz ready-to-eat dried apricots
1 tsp clear honey
salt

to serve
*50g/2oz blanched almonds, fried in butter
  until browned*
chopped fresh coriander

Couscous goes well with the North African flavours of this dish.

1 Soak the chickpeas overnight. Drain, tip into a saucepan and cover generously with fresh cold water. Bring to the boil, simmer for 45 minutes and drain.

2 Heat the oil in a large casserole and brown the lamb all over. Remove and set aside. Pour off most of the fat, leaving 1 tablespoon in the dish, add the onions and fry for 8-10 minutes until soft.

3 Preheat the oven to 160°C/325°F/Gas 3. Mix together the ginger, garlic, chillies, cumin, coriander, pepper and paprika. Add half of this to the onions, tip in the tomatoes and cook for 2-3 minutes. Put in the lamb and chickpeas, cover generously with water (about 850ml/1¹/2 pints), bring to the boil and leave to simmer for 5 minutes.

4 Cover and cook in the oven for 1¹/2–2 hours until the chickpeas are really tender. (You can prepare up to this stage the day before. Allow to cool, cover and refrigerate. Bring back to simmering point before starting the next step.)

5 Remove from the oven and stir in the remaining spice mixture, the saffron and cinnamon, carrots, apricots, honey and salt to taste. Cover and return to the oven for 45 minutes to 1 hour, until the lamb is tender and the vegetables cooked.

6 Scatter the almonds and coriander on top to serve.

braised partridge with cabbage

Preparation 35 minutes
Cooking 1¹/₂ hours

salt and pepper
1 Savoy cabbage (about 1kg/2¹/₄lb), cored
and cut into wedges
4 partridges, cleaned and trussed
2 tbsp vegetable oil
6 thick slices of streaky bacon
1 tbsp juniper berries, crushed
3 carrots, cut into 1cm/¹/₂in slices
125ml/4fl oz dry white wine
200ml/7fl oz chicken stock
1 onion
1 clove
bouquet garni (made with parsley stems, a
bay leaf and thyme)
1 tsp cornflour
2 tbsp chopped fresh parsley

This is a favourite recipe in northern Burgundy.

1 Preheat the oven to 180°C/375°F/Gas 4. Bring a large pan of salted water to the boil and add the cabbage wedges. Leave to simmer for 5 minutes until almost tender, then drain and rinse under cold water. Set aside. Season the partridges.

2 Heat the oil in a large ovenproof casserole and add the partridges. Cook for 10 minutes until browned on all sides. Remove them from the pan and set aside.

3 Allow the casserole to cool slightly, then line the base with the bacon slices. Add half the cooked cabbage, the crushed juniper berries and season well with salt and pepper. Put the partridges on top and surround with the carrots. Cover with the remaining cabbage. Season again and pour over the wine and stock. Stud the onion with the clove. Make a cross in the onion, cutting halfway through so it opens out slightly. Add the onion and bouquet garni to the casserole, pushing them well down into the cabbage.

4 Cover the casserole and cook in the oven for about 1¹/₄ hours, or until the partridges and carrots are tender.

5 Transfer the partridges to a chopping board and cover with foil to keep warm. Using a slotted spoon, arrange the vegetables and bacon in a serving dish, leaving the juices behind in the casserole. Discard the bouquet garni.

6 Put the casserole over a high heat and bring the juices to the boil. Leave to simmer for about 15 minutes to reduce by half. Stir a tablespoon of water into the cornflour and mix to a paste. Whisk this into the juices and stir the sauce until smooth and thickened. Season to taste.

7 Arrange the partridges on top of the vegetables. Pour over the sauce and sprinkle with the chopped parsley. Serve with mashed potatoes.

Variation
For a more economical dish, this recipe can be made with 2 small birds and stretched far enough to feed 4 by adding 8 small sausages. At the end of step 2, fry the sausages in the pan for 5 minutes until brown. Remove and set aside with the partridges. Add them to the casserole about 15 minutes before the end of the cooking time.

garlic chicken with herbed potatoes

**Preparation about 15 minutes, plus
   2 hours' or overnight marinating
Cooking about 1 hour**

*8–12 chicken drumsticks and/or thighs,
   on the bone and with skin on*
4 heads of green garlic (see introduction)
*1kg/2¹/₄lb salad potatoes, such as
   Charlotte or Nicola*
2 tbsp chopped parsley

for the marinade
8 tbsp olive oil
2 tsp Dijon mustard
1 tbsp balsamic vinegar
1 tsp chopped fresh thyme
4–8 sprigs of rosemary, lightly crushed
salt and pepper
a few pinches of light muscovado sugar
2 unwaxed lemons

*This is a simple dish that still impresses. If you can only find ordinary garlic, bear in
mind that the flavour is stronger and less sweet, so you may want to cut the quantity.*

1 First make the marinade by whisking together the oil, mustard, vinegar and herbs.
Season with black pepper and a large pinch or two of sugar. Cut the lemons in half,
finely grate the zest of one half and reserve. Squeeze the juice from that into the
marinade. Put the chicken in a non-metallic dish and spoon the marinade over it.
Add the remaining lemon halves and leave to marinate until ready to cook. (This
can be done up to 2 hours ahead or overnight if that suits you better.)

2 Just over an hour before you want to eat, preheat the oven to 200°C/400°F/
Gas 6. Cut a thin slice off the top of the garlic (this makes it easier to squeeze it out
later) and halve the potatoes or cut them into largish chunks, depending on size.
Drain most of the marinade into a roasting tin and add the potatoes and garlic,
tossing to coat them in the oil. Roast, uncovered, for about 20 minutes.

3 Add the chicken, rosemary and lemon to the tin, scraping in any bits of marinade.
Toss to mix, arrange the chicken skin-side up and season well with salt. Roast for
40-45 minutes, or until the potatoes are cooked and the chicken is golden and crisp.

4 Mix the lemon zest and parsley, scatter over the chicken and serve immediately.

quick beef stroganoff

Preparation about 15 minutes
Cooking about 20 minutes

knob of butter
1 tbsp vegetable oil
1 large onion, sliced
500g/1lb 2oz rump steak
2 tbsp plain flour
salt and pepper
2 tbsp paprika, plus extra for sprinkling
250g/9oz chestnut mushrooms
200ml/7fl oz beef stock
2 tbsp white wine vinegar
284ml/¹/₂ pint carton of soured cream
boiled rice or noodles, to serve

As this dish makes expensive steak go further, it is perfect for midweek entertaining.

1 Heat the butter and oil in a large frying pan. Cook the sliced onion in this for 5 minutes until softened.

2 Meanwhile, cut the beef into thin strips. Season the flour with salt, pepper and paprika, then toss in the beef to coat lightly, shaking off any excess.

3 Add the beef to the pan and cook for 3-4 minutes until starting to brown. Halve the mushrooms, add to the pan and stir-fry for a couple of minutes. Pour in the stock and vinegar, bring to the boil, then lower the heat and simmer gently for 5 minutes.

4 Stir the soured cream into the pan and cook gently for 1 minute, without boiling (if the mixture boils it will curdle), then season to taste.

5 Spoon the stroganoff on to a bed of steamed rice or lightly buttered noodles and sprinkle with a little extra paprika.

coq au vin

Serves 4-6
Preparation 50-60 minutes, plus cooling and 1-3 days' marinating
Cooking 80-90 minutes

1 roasting chicken, about 2.25kg/5lb, cut into 8 pieces
1 tbsp vegetable oil
175g/6oz chopped rindless smoked bacon or lardons
500ml/16fl oz chicken stock, plus more if needed
salt and pepper
2 shallots, chopped
2 garlic cloves, chopped
bouquet garni (tied sprigs of bay leaves, thyme and parsley)
25g/1oz butter
18–20 baby onions or small shallots, peeled
250g/9oz button mushrooms, trimmed and quartered
1 tbsp chopped parsley

for the marinade
1 onion, sliced
1 carrot, sliced
2 celery stalks, sliced
1 garlic clove, peeled
1 tsp black peppercorns
75cl bottle of red wine
2 tbsp olive oil

for the beurre manié
25g/1oz softened butter
25g/1oz plain flour

To soak up the sauce for coq au vin, *boiled potatoes or noodles are traditional, together with fried bead croûtes.*

1 At least a day ahead, make the marinade by combining all the ingredients, except the olive oil, in a saucepan. Bring to the boil and simmer for 5 minutes. Let it cool completely.

2 Pack the chicken in a deep non-metallic bowl, add the marinade and spoon the olive oil on top to keep the chicken moist. Cover and chill for 1-3 days, turning the pieces from time to time.

3 Remove the chicken pieces from the marinade and pat dry with kitchen paper. Strain the marinade, reserving the vegetables separately.

4 Heat the vegetable oil in a flameproof casserole and fry the bacon until browned and the fat runs. Scoop out the bacon, leaving the fat. Add the chicken in batches, skin down. Brown well over a medium heat for at least 10 minutes. Turn, brown the other side and remove from the pan.

5 Add the reserved marinade vegetables to the casserole. Fry until starting to brown, 5-7 minutes. Pour in the marinade liquid, bring to the boil and simmer for 5 minutes. Add the stock, season and then add the chopped shallots, garlic and bouquet garni. Add the chicken, pushing it into the sauce. Cover and simmer until the pieces feel tender when pierced with a fork, 45-60 minutes.

6 While that cooks, melt the 25g/1oz butter in a pan and add the baby onions. Brown for 5-7 minutes, shaking every so often. Remove and set aside. Add the mushrooms and fry until tender, 3-5 minutes. Set aside with the bacon.

7 To make the beurre manié, mash together the butter and flour with a fork.

8 When the chicken is cooked, strain the sauce and discard the vegetables. Wipe out the casserole, add the sauce and bring to a simmer. Add the beurre manié a little at a time, whisking thoroughly between each addition to prevent lumps. Add the onions and simmer for 5-8 minutes, until almost tender. Add the bacon and mushrooms, and simmer for 3-5 minutes.

9 Replace the chicken and gently heat for 3-5 minutes. Adjust the seasoning. Transfer to a serving dish or serve in the casserole, sprinkled with parsley.

cosy feasts for two

On occasion, you'll want to share that sense of comfort with a special person, be it a partner or someone new in your life. Here are some dishes that will help produce the necessary easy and intimate atmosphere.

Mediterranean chicken with rocket and potato crush

Chicken breasts are baked with moist goats' cheese, garlic and zingy roasted peppers, then served with a crush of potatoes, garlic and rocket on the side, for a dish that's so simple but packed with flavour.

Preparation 15 minutes
Cooking 40 minutes

3 plump garlic cloves, peeled
3 tbsp chopped fresh parsley
3 tbsp olive oil
2 boneless, skinless chicken breasts, preferably organic
100g/4oz goats' cheese
3 strips of roasted peppers in oil, drained, each cut in half
a few sprigs of fresh thyme
salt and pepper
300g/10oz small new potatoes
85g/3oz packet rocket or watercress, tough stems removed

1 Preheat the oven to 200°C/400°F/ Gas 6. Simmer the garlic cloves in a little boiling water for 4–5 minutes, until just softened. Drain and chop them. Mix with the parsley and 1 tablespoon of the oil.
2 Make 3 diagonal slits across the width of each chicken breast, three-quarters of the way down. Put half the garlic mixture aside and spread the rest over the chicken and into the slits.
3 Cut the cheese into 6 rounds. Halve each slice and tuck 2 halves, a piece of pepper and some thyme into each slit. Season and put into a lightly oiled, shallow ovenproof dish. Bake for 30 minutes, or until the chicken is cooked.
4 While the chicken bakes, cook the potatoes in boiling salted water for about 15 minutes until tender. Drain, return them to the pan and coarsely crush with a fork. Stir in the rocket and let it wilt in the heat of the pan. Stir the remaining oil into the reserved garlic mixture, season with salt and pepper and stir into the potatoes.
5 Serve the potatoes with the chicken, with any chicken juices poured around.

duck with lime, ginger and honey

Roast some sweet potatoes and lime wedges with the duck, and serve with stir-fried pak choy.

Preparation 20 minutes
Cooking 1 hour 40 minutes, plus 15 minutes' resting

7.5cm/3in piece of unpeeled fresh root ginger
1 oven-ready duck, about 1.8kg/4lb
3 limes
4 star anise
1 small onion, peeled and halved
1 tbsp dark soy sauce, plus extra to taste
2 tbsp clear honey, plus extra to taste
300–450ml/½–¾ pint duck or chicken stock

1 Slice half the unpeeled ginger. Preheat the oven to 200°C/400°F/ Gas 6. Wash and dry the duck, then prick the skin and season inside and out. Halve 1 lime, squeeze the juice into the cavity and put in the halves with the ginger slices, 2 star anise and the onion.

2 Put the duck, breast down, on a rack in a roasting tin and roast, uncovered, for 40 minutes. Reduce the heat to 190°C/375°F/Gas 5, turn the duck over and roast for another 20 minutes.
3 Meanwhile, zest the remaining limes and peel the remaining ginger. Shred both and blanch for 3 minutes in boiling water. Drain and refresh under cold running water. Mix the soy sauce, 2 tablespoons of honey, 1 tablespoon of stock and the juice of 1 lime to make a glaze.
4 Pour all but 1 tablespoon of fat from the tin. Brush the duck with half the glaze. Add 300ml/½ pint stock and roast for 30 minutes, brushing with more glaze halfway through. The duck will be dark brown and shiny, with clear juices (push a skewer in the thick part of a leg). Allow to rest on a cutting board for 15 minutes, loosely covered with foil.
5 Put the roasting tin on the stove. Add the rest of the glaze, star anise, stock and the cavity juices. Boil for 2-3 minutes to reduce and thicken. Strain into a pan. Add the shredded ginger and lime zest. Simmer for 2-3 minutes, then season to taste. Serve with the duck.

creamy mussels with cider and bacon

Preparation 30-35 minutes
Cooking 30-35 minutes

*225g/8oz Charlotte potatoes, scrubbed
    and cut in half if large*
salt and pepper
*½ small Savoy cabbage (about
    350g/12oz), cored and shredded*
1 tbsp olive oil
2 shallots, finely chopped
1 garlic clove, crushed
200ml/7fl oz dry cider
a few sprigs of parsley
a few sprigs of thyme
1 bay leaf
*1kg/2¼lb fresh mussels, well scrubbed
    and beards removed*
*85g/3oz diced pancetta or rindless streaky
    bacon*
2 tbsp half-fat crème fraîche
knob of chilled butter, cut into pieces

1 Cook the potatoes in a large saucepan of salted boiled water for 12-15 minutes until tender, adding the cabbage for the last 2 minutes.
2 While the potatoes are cooking, heat the oil in a medium saucepan with a tight-fitting lid. Add the shallots and garlic, lower the heat and cook for 2 minutes. Pour in the cider, add the herbs and bay, and season with pepper. Increase the heat and bring to the boil, then tip in the mussels and cover tightly. Cook for 5-8 minutes, shaking frequently, until the mussels open.
3 While they are cooking, put a small frying pan over a moderately high heat and dry-fry the pancetta or bacon for 3 minutes, stirring frequently until tender and crisp. Tip on to kitchen paper and leave to drain.
4 Drain the potatoes and cabbage well and pat dry with kitchen paper. (The potatoes and cabbage can be prepared ahead to this stage and reheated in the microwave before serving.) When the mussels are open, put a colander over a clean saucepan and pour the mussels and liquid into the colander. Throw out any mussels that haven't opened, together with the sprigs of herbs and the bay leaf.
5 Place the pan of cooking liquid over a moderate heat and stir in the crème fraîche. Gently simmer, whisking in the butter a little at a time. Remove from the heat and season.
6 Divide the potatoes and cabbage between 2 warmed bowls, top with mussels, followed by the cooking liquid. Scatter with pancetta or bacon and serve.

Meat-free
comforters

A MEAL DOESN'T HAVE TO CONSIST OF 'MEAT AND TWO
VEG' TO BE SATISFYING. SOME OF THE MOST
COMFORTING DISHES HAVE A PREDOMINANTLY
VEGETABLE BASE, IN CLASSICALLY WARMING CONTEXTS
LIKE PASTA SAUCES AND BAKES, CRISP BAKED PIZZAS,
TANGY CHEESY OMELETTES AND SPICY CURRIES.

spinach rolls with feta

Makes 12 pastries
Preparation 30 minutes
Cooking about 35 minutes

100g/4oz butter
5 tbsp olive oil
1 large leek, trimmed, thinly sliced and
thoroughly washed
500g/1lb 2oz large-leaf spinach, washed,
drained and shredded (including the
stems)
3 tbsp finely chopped fresh dill (including
the stems)
400g/14oz Greek feta cheese, crumbled
salt and pepper
2 medium eggs
3 tbsp milk
24 sheets of filo pastry, total weight about
750g/1lb 10oz

Called spanakopita, *these rolls can be served warm or cold, with a crisp salad.*

1 Melt 25g/1oz of the butter with 1 tablespoon of the oil in a saucepan. Add the leek, cover and cook over a medium heat for about 10 minutes until soft but not coloured, stirring to prevent sticking. Remove from the heat and leave to cool.

2 Preheat the oven to 180°C/350°F/Gas 4. Put the spinach in a very large mixing bowl and add the dill, feta, remaining olive oil, salt and pepper, and 1 of the eggs, beaten. Add the leek and mix thoroughly with your hands.

3 Melt the remaining butter in a pan. Make an egg wash with the remaining egg and the milk. Remove the filo from the fridge and cover it with a damp cloth. You are now ready to assemble the dish. Take a sheet of filo and brush it with some melted butter. Dip another brush in the egg wash and brush this over the butter. Put another sheet of filo on top and repeat the coats of melted butter and egg wash. Spread about 100g/4oz of the spinach mixture over the filo, leaving a clean edge of 2.5cm/1in all around for folding. Sprinkle some egg wash over the spinach, then fold over the longest sides of the filo. Roll the filo up from one short end like a fat cigar, then put the roll in a baking dish with the loose end of the filo underneath. Repeat to make 12 pastries in total, arranging the rolls close together in the dish.

4 Bake for 20-25 minutes, until the filo is lightly golden - it doesn't go darker.

cheesy sweet potato and cauliflower

Preparation about 10 minutes
Cooking about 20-25 minutes

2 large orange-fleshed sweet potatoes
1 small cauliflower, broken into large
florets
5 tbsp milk
300g/10½oz ready-made cheese
sauce (or see page 18)
3 tbsp snipped fresh chives
salt and pepper
85g/3oz Cheddar cheese, grated

1 Cook the sweet potatoes whole with their skins on High in the microwave for 10-15 minutes until tender. Set aside. Put the cauliflower in a microwavable bowl with a good splash of water. Cover with plastic film and microwave for 5 minutes on High.

2 Preheat the grill. Cut the sweet potatoes into wedges and lay them in the bottom of an ovenproof dish. Drain the cauliflower florets and spoon them over the potatoes. Stir the milk into the cheese sauce, then warm in the microwave according to the instructions on the tub. Stir in the chives, adjust the seasoning, then pour over the cauliflower and potatoes. Sprinkle with the grated cheese.

3 Grill for 3-4 minutes, until golden and bubbling.

Variation
If you don't have a microwave, simply boil both the sweet potatoes and cauliflower in separate pans, about 20-30 minutes for the potatoes and 12-15 minutes for the cauliflower, and heat the sauce gently on the stove.

Preparation 35-40 minutes
Cooking about 30 minutes

pinch of saffron strands
3 star anise
8 green cardamom pods
1 tsp fennel seeds
2 pieces of mace (optional)
1 tsp turmeric
225g/8oz basmati rice
salt
25g/1oz butter or ghee or 1 tbsp vegetable
*   oil*
225g/8oz mixed wild mushrooms, sliced
*   if large*

for the herb paste
large handful of fresh mint
large handful of fresh coriander
large handful of fresh basil
6 tbsp natural yoghurt
1 garlic clove, halved
2 small, thin green chillies, deseeded and
*   roughly chopped*

for the roasted spices
seeds from 5 cardamom pods
1/2 tsp fennel seeds
1/4 tsp ground mace

for the pastry
250g/9oz puff pastry, defrosted if frozen
a few fennel or pumpkin seeds
ground coriander

mushroom biryani

1 Put the saffron in a bowl with 3 tablespoons of water. Half fill a pan with water, add the star anise, cardamom, fennel seeds, mace if using and the turmeric. Bring to the boil, add the rice and boil for 8 minutes until almost tender. Drain the rice, then season with salt and the saffron water. Set aside.

2 While the rice is cooking, make the herb paste: in a blender, blitz all the ingredients until smooth. Add salt to taste.

3 Make the roasted spices: grind the fennel and cardamom, and stir in the mace. Put the spices in a hot dry pan and cook, stirring, until lightly toasted.

4 Heat the butter, ghee or oil in a frying pan, add the mushrooms and toss for about 1 minute over a high heat. Stir in the herb paste and roasted spices. Set aside.

5 Preheat the oven to 200°C/400°F/Gas 6. Roll out the pastry so that it is large enough to cover a 1.2 litre/2 pint, 20cm/8in round pie dish. Scatter the fennel or pumpkin seeds and a pinch of ground coriander over the top, then use a rolling pin to press them into the pastry.

6 Spoon the rice into the pie dish, dampen the rim, then cover with the pastry lid, pressing to secure. Bake for 20 minutes until the pastry is risen and golden.

red onion and goats' cheese tart

Serves 4-6
Preparation 15 minutes
Cooking 45 minutes

500g/1lb 2 oz pack of ready-made
shortcrust pastry, defrosted if frozen
flour, for dusting
4 red onions
4 tbsp olive oil
4–5 sprigs of fresh thyme or 1 tsp dried
100g/4oz black olives
100g/4oz firm goats' cheese

1 Preheat the oven to 200°C/400°F/Gas 6. Roll out the pastry and use to line a 23x33cm/9x13in Swiss roll tin, trimming off the excess. Chill the base while you make the filling.

2 Thinly slice the onions. Heat the olive oil in a large pan, add the onions and gently cook for 10 minutes. Stir in the thyme (if using fresh, reserve a few sprigs to garnish) and cook for a further 5 minutes, until the onions are very soft and lightly browned.

3 Spread the onions and their juices over the pastry case, then dot with the olives and crumble over the goats' cheese. Bake for 25–30 minutes, until the pastry is crisp and the cheese golden.

4 Allow the tart to cool for 5 minutes and garnish it with some fresh thyme, if using, before cutting.

Florentine pizza

Preparation about 15 minutes
Cooking about 20 minutes

30cm/12in bought pizza base (preferably deep and crispy)
6 rounded tbsp tomato sauce (bought or see page 100)
175g/6oz spinach leaves
100g/4oz antipasti mushrooms from a jar
salt and pepper
50g/2oz Parmesan cheese, finely grated
4 medium eggs

1 Preheat the oven to 200°C/400°F/Gas 6. Put the pizza base on a baking sheet and spread with the sauce.

2 Put the spinach in a microwavable bowl, cover with cling film and pierce it a couple of times. Put in the microwave on High for 2 minutes until wilted. Alternatively, cook the spinach in a covered pan for 2-3 minutes.

3 Drain well, squeezing out excess liquid. Spread the spinach on the pizza base. Scatter the mushrooms over the top. Season, sprinkle with half the cheese, then bake for 10 minutes.

4 Make 4 hollows in the spinach with the back of a spoon and crack an egg into each. Sprinkle with the remaining cheese and bake for a further 6-8 minutes, until the eggs are just set.

courgette, tomato and basil tart

Serves 4-6
Preparation 25-35 minutes
Cooking about 1 hour

250g/9oz ready-made shortcrust pastry
flour, for dusting
2 courgettes, sliced at an angle
1 tbsp olive oil
salt and pepper
300g/12oz cooked new potatoes, sliced
500g/1lb 2oz tomatoes, sliced
100g/4oz Gruyère cheese, grated
handful of basil leaves
3 eggs
200m/7fl oz crème fraîche
150ml/¼ pint milk
4 tbsp grated Parmesan cheese

1 Preheat the oven to 200°C/400°F/Gas 6. Roll out the pastry to a 30cm/12in round and use it to line a deepish, loose-based tart tin. Allow the pastry to hang over the edge of the tin and only trim it if it overhangs too much. If you have the time, chill the pastry for 20 minutes.

2 Line the pastry case with greaseproof paper and fill with baking beans. Bake for 15 minutes, then remove the paper and beans, and bake for a further 5 minutes, until the pastry is pale golden. Reduce the oven setting to 180°C/350°F/Gas 4.

3 Lightly brush the courgette slices with oil and season. Griddle or fry in a non-stick frying pan until lightly browned on each side. Remove from the pan and leave to cool. Layer half the potatoes, courgettes and tomatoes in the pastry case. Season each layer and sprinkle it with a little Gruyère and a few basil leaves. Repeat the layers, finishing with tomatoes. Beat together the eggs, crème fraîche and milk. Season, then stir in the remaining Gruyère and half the Parmesan. Pour this over the filling and sprinkle with the rest of the Parmesan.

4 Bake for 35-45 minutes, until golden and firm to the touch. Scatter with the remaining basil and allow to cool for 10 minutes before serving.

Preparation 30 minutes
Cooking 45 minutes

5 tbsp fruity olive oil
750g/1lb 10oz ripe cherry tomatoes
2 tsp dried oregano
2 tsp sugar
salt and pepper
225g/8oz soft rindless goats' cheese, such
*   as full-fat soft organic Welsh goats'*
*   cheese*
6 tbsp fresh red or green pesto
12 sheets of fresh lasagne
350g/12oz ripe vine tomatoes, thinly
*   sliced (you need 24 slices)*
3 tbsp freshly grated Parmesan (optional)
basil leaves, to dress

goats' cheese and pesto cannelloni

1 Preheat the oven to 220°C/425°F/Gas 7 and lightly oil a 20x25cm/8x10in baking dish. Halve 250g/9oz of the cherry tomatoes and set aside.

2 Heat the remaining oil in a frying pan, add the remaining cherry tomatoes (they will splutter a little) and cover tightly. Cook over a high heat, shaking the pan occasionally, for 5 minutes until the tomatoes start to break down. Uncover and stir in the oregano, sugar, salt and pepper. Set aside.

3 Soften the cheese in a bowl and beat in the pesto. Lay the lasagne sheets on a work surface and spread the cheese mixture evenly over them. Lay 2 tomato slices on each sheet, season well and roll each up from the narrow side like a Swiss roll.

4 Spoon half the tomato sauce over the base of the dish. Arrange the pasta rolls over the sauce, then spoon over the remaining sauce. Scatter the reserved cherry tomato halves on top and cover with foil. Bake for 25-30 minutes.

5 Remove the foil, sprinkle with the Parmesan if using, and bake for a further 10 minutes until beginning to brown. Remove from the oven and allow to stand for 10 minutes before serving. Scatter with basil leaves and serve with a crisp green salad.

mushroom and goats' cheese polenta pie

Serves 6
Preparation 45 minutes
Cooking time 35 minutes

850ml/1½ pints boiling vegetable stock
175g/6oz quick-cook polenta
225g/8oz firm goats' cheese
50g/2oz grated fresh Parmesan cheese
4 tbsp chopped fresh parsley
salt and pepper
3 tbsp olive oil, plus more for greasing
25g/1oz butter
450g/1lb mixed cultivated and wild
*   mushrooms*
1 large or 2 small red onions, cut into thin
*   wedges*
1 tsp light muscovado sugar
1 celery stalk, sliced
2 tbsp ruby port
285g/10oz jar of roasted red peppers,
*   drained*
200g/7oz vacuum-packed cooked and
*   peeled chestnuts*
1 tbsp wholegrain mustard
1 tbsp fresh thyme leaves or 1 tsp dried
142ml/¼pint carton of double cream

1 Add the polenta to 700ml/1¼ pints of boiling stock in a steady stream, stirring. Reduce the heat and cook for 1 minute, stirring. Crumble in half the goats' cheese, half the Parmesan, and half the parsley, and season. Transfer to a 20x30cm/8x12in oiled tin (it should be about 1cm/½in deep). Leave until set and prepare the filling.

2 Preheat the oven to 190°C/375°F/Gas 5. Heat the butter and 2 tablespoons of the oil in a heavy pan. Fry the mushrooms for 4-5 minutes, remove and set aside. Add the remaining oil to the pan and cook the onions for 15 minutes until golden. Stir in the sugar and cook for 5 minutes. Add the celery and fry for 2-3 minutes. Return the mushrooms to the pan, add the port and deglaze. Add the remaining stock and simmer for 1 minute. Add the remaining parsley, the peppers, chestnuts, mustard, thyme and cream, and simmer for 2 minutes. Crumble in the rest of the goats' cheese. Season.

3 Spoon into a 25x15x4cm/10x6x1½in ovenproof dish. Divide the polenta into 16 slices by cutting it lengthwise in half, then each half across into 8. Arrange the filling on top and sprinkle with the remaining Parmesan. Set aside for up to 4 hours.

4 Bake for 30 minutes, then finish by grilling for 5-8 minutes until golden.

grilled vegetable couscous with halumi

Preparation 20-25 minutes
Cooking about 5 minutes

200g/7oz couscous
300ml/¹/₂ pint hot vegetable stock
5 tbsp olive oil
2 tbsp lemon juice
1 garlic clove, finely chopped
2 red peppers, deseeded and each cut into
*   6 pieces*
1 aubergine, cut into chunks
250g/9oz halumi cheese, sliced into 8
*   pieces*
2 tbsp toasted flaked almonds
1 tbsp pesto sauce

1 Put the couscous in a bowl and pour in the hot vegetable stock. Set aside.

2 Mix together the oil, lemon and garlic, then brush a little of this over the peppers and aubergine. Spread the vegetables on the barbecue or grill and cook for 2-3 minutes on each side, until softened and slightly charred.

3 Brush the halumi with some of the lemon and garlic oil and cook on the barbecue or under a hot grill for a minute or so on each side until golden.

4 When the couscous has absorbed all the stock, fluff it up with a fork. Spoon on to a serving plate and scatter over the aubergine, peppers, halumi and toasted almonds. Mix the pesto into the remaining lemon and garlic oil and drizzle over the vegetables and cheese.

creamy rosemary and butternut squash pasta

Preparation about 15 minutes
Cooking about 35 minutes

1 tbsp olive oil
25g/1oz butter
700g/1lb 9oz butternut squash
4 sprigs of fresh rosemary or ¹/₂ tsp dried
salt and pepper
175g/6oz chestnut mushrooms, sliced
300g/10oz penne or rigatoni
250g/9oz tub of mascarpone cheese
freshly grated Parmesan cheese, to serve

1 Preheat the oven to 200°C/400°F/Gas 6. Put the oil and butter in a roasting tin and place in the oven to heat. Meanwhile, peel the squash and cut into bite-sized chunks. Toss into the melted butter and oil, together with the rosemary, salt and pepper.

2 Roast the squash for 25 minutes, then stir in the mushrooms and return to the oven for 10 minutes.

3 Meanwhile, cook the pasta in boiling salted waster until just tender, using the packet instructions as a guide.

4 Put the roasting tin with the squash mixture on the stove. Stir in a couple of tablespoons of the pasta cooking water, then stir in the mascarpone and heat through until bubbling. Drain the pasta and stir in, then taste and add more seasoning if necessary.

5 Serve each portion sprinkled with freshly grated Parmesan. This goes well with a watercress salad.

pasta with cauliflower, broccoli and chard

Preparation 15 minutes
Cooking time 40 minutes

350g/12oz dried pasta ribbons
175g/6oz cauliflower, cut into florets
175g/6oz broccoli, cut into florets
120g/4oz baby chard
a little olive oil
freshly grated Parmesan cheese, to serve

for the tomato sauce
2 tsp olive oil
1 onion, chopped
1 garlic clove, finely chopped
400g/14oz can of chopped tomatoes
150ml/¼ pint vegetable stock
1 tsp dried oregano
3 tbsp chopped fresh parsley
salt and pepper

You could use spinach leaves instead of chard in this recipe.

1 First make the sauce: heat the oil in a heavy pan and fry the onion gently until just translucent. Add the garlic and fry for 1 more minute. Stir in the tomatoes, stock and herbs. Simmer for about 25 minutes until thick, then season.

2 Bring a large pan of salted water to the boil and cook the pasta until just tender, 8–10 minutes, or according to packet instructions.

3 Meanwhile, cook the cauliflower in another pan for 6 minutes, add the broccoli and cook for 3–4 minutes, until both are just tender. Drain well and keep warm.

4 Drain the pasta well and stir in the chard with a little olive oil and seasoning to taste – the leaves will wilt nicely from the heat of the pasta.

5 Toss the pasta and chard with the broccoli, cauliflower and tomato sauce and spoon into warmed serving bowls. Serve immediately with grated Parmesan.

chive and brie omelette

Serves 1
Preparation 5 minutes
Cooking 2-3 minutes

3 large eggs
salt and pepper
2 tbsp roughly snipped fresh chives
knob of butter
85g/3oz Brie, rind left on, cut into cubes
about the size of large dice

1 In a bowl, lightly beat the eggs for about 20 seconds, until the yolks are broken and just mixed into the whites. Do not beat them any more, or you will have a tough, chewy omelette. Season and sprinkle in the chives.

2 Heat a frying pan, drop in the knob of butter and, when it sizzles, swirl it around to coat the pan. Turn down the heat slightly and pour in the eggs. Swirl the pan again so the eggs are spread out evenly. As they start to cook, they will look opaque and paler, 15-20 seconds. Using a spatula, draw the edges of the omelette into the centre of the pan, allowing pools of the raw egg to run into the spaces created.

3 After about 1-1½ minutes the omelette will be set. The surface should still look soft and even slightly liquid – soft, silky and melting in texture. Scatter over the cubes of Brie.

4 Using a spatula, fold one-third of the omelette carefully into the middle. Fold over the other edge, then slide on to a plate. Serve with a green salad.

storecupboard solace

Some people seem to think that it always involves much more planning to produce a meat-free meal, but this just isn't the case. Here are some simple but deeply satisfying dishes you can make with the contents of your storecupboard and whatever veg and herbs are left in the drawer.

parsley and walnut pesto pasta

Preparation 5 minutes

1 plump garlic clove
50g/2oz walnut pieces
large handful of fresh parsley, including
    stalks (about 85g/3oz)
2 tbsp sun-dried tomato paste or sun-dried
    tomatoes in oil, roughly chopped
1 tbsp pine nuts
3 tbsp olive oil
25g/1oz freshly grated Parmesan cheese
salt and pepper
500g/1lb 2oz cooked spaghetti, to serve
chopped parsley leaves, to serve

1 Whiz all the ingredients except the Parmesan in a food processor to make a coarse paste. Stir in the Parmesan and season to taste. Toss with the cooked spaghetti and serve scattered with chopped parsley leaves.

Variation
If you haven't got any parsley to hand, you can use any of the variety of herbs and leaves that can nowadays be found in sachets in corner shops. Try torn basil leaves, chopped chives, rocket, shredded watercress or baby spinach leaves.

leek and pepper pizzas

Preparation 10 minutes
Cooking 25–30 minutes

290g/10oz packet of bread mix
1 tbsp olive oil, plus extra for greasing
2 large leeks, sliced
3 large red peppers, deseeded and cut into
    chunks
100ml/3¹/₂fl oz canned or bottled tomato
    sauce
50g/2oz sultanas
25g/1oz pine nuts
a few rosemary sprigs, to serve (optional)

1 Preheat the oven to 220°C/425°F/ Gas 7. Make up the bread mix according to the packet instructions. Divide the dough into 4. On a lightly floured surface, roll each piece out into a 20cm/8in circle. Very lightly grease 1 or 2 baking sheets and put the pizza bases on them.

2 Heat the oil in a large frying pan and stir in the leeks and peppers. Fry briefly until well coated in oil and slightly softened. Set aside.

3 Spoon the tomato sauce over the pizza bases, leaving a clear edge, then spoon the leek and pepper mixture on top. Sprinkle over the sultanas and pine nuts.

4 Bake for 12–15 minutes, until the bases are crisp and well coloured and the topping vegetables are cooked. If you have them, top each with a sprig or two of rosemary before serving.

Variation
You can make this sort of pizza with a wide variety of vegetables that happen to be left in your fridge or vegetable basket. Try sliced cooked new potatoes with gently browned onion and crumbled blue cheese, broccoli with goats' cheese, red onions with black olives and capers, carrots and fennel with chopped garlic and Parmesan. Go on, experiment!

posh beans on toast

Baked beans are not only our favourite convenience food and incredibly comforting, they are also very good for you, provided you buy the low-salt, low-sugar type. Whenever you want a satisfying last-minute snack, there are endless ways of tricking them up to make them more special.

Serves 1
Preparation 5 minutes
Cooking 5 minutes

1 small (150g/5oz) can of baked beans
1 teaspoon wholegrain mustard
pepper
1 or 2 slices of bread
knob of butter
dollop of crème fraîche
handful of grated Cheddar cheese

1 Heat the beans in a small pan and stir in the mustard with pepper to taste.
2 Toast the bread and butter it thickly. Pile the hot beans on the buttered toast, top with the crème fraîche and the cheese, then season with more black pepper.
3 Eat immediately.

Variation
Try adding a chopped deseeded red pepper, some chopped spring or red onion, chilli powder to taste and a squirt of lime juice for chilli beans.

Perk-up
puds

THE SWEET COURSE IS ALMOST BY DEFINITION
COMFORT FOOD – ALTHOUGH FEW WOULD DISPUTE
THAT A STICKY PUDDING OR AN ICE CREAM PROVIDES
INFINITELY MORE SOLACE THAN A FRUIT SALAD.
HOWEVER, IT IS NOT JUST THE SWEETNESS THAT
MAKES PUDDINGS SO COMFORTING, IT IS THE LOVELY
RANGE OF SOOTHING TEXTURES THEY EMPLOY, LIKE
THE CRUNCH OF PASTRY, THE SILKINESS OF CREAM –
AND, OF COURSE, THE LINGERING DARK
JOYS OF CHOCOLATE.

oatmeal praline ice cream

Serves 8
Preparation 20 minutes, plus
softening and freezing
Cooking 10 minutes

1 tub of quality vanilla ice cream

for the praline
150g/5oz pinhead oatmeal
vegetable oil, for greasing
150g/5oz liquid glucose syrup
100g/4oz caster sugar

1 First make the praline: preheat the grill and toast the oatmeal for a couple of minutes, watching it very carefully and turning it frequently so it does not burn. It is ready when it smells nutty and toasty. Tip it on to an oiled baking sheet.

2 Put the glucose and sugar in a heavy-based pan and stir over a low heat until the sugar dissolves. Dip a pastry brush in cold water and quickly brush down the inside of the pan to loosen any sugar that is stuck to the sides. Then, without stirring, allow the mixture to bubble away for 8–10 minutes or until it is golden brown in colour, swirling the pan around a couple of times.

3 Pour the mixture over the oats. Try to cover them all, but don't worry if you can't. Leave to cool, then break up and place in a food processor with any uncovered oats. Using the pulse button, blend briefly. Do not overprocess or it will be too powdery - you want good chunks of praline.

4 Allow the ice cream to soften slightly, then stir in the praline. Refreeze until required. It will freeze for up to 2 weeks.

spiced plum squares

Cuts into 12 squares
Preparation 20 minutes
Cooking 20 minutes

150g/6oz butter, cut into pieces, plus
*   more for greasing*
300g/10oz self-raising flour, plus more
*   for dusting*
50g/2oz caster sugar
finely grated zest and juice of 1 orange
about 150ml/¼ pint milk
700g/1½lb plums, stoned and quartered
50g/2oz butter
50g/2oz light muscovado sugar
1 tsp ground cinnamon
icing sugar, for dusting
cream or crème fraîche, to serve

1 Preheat the oven to 200°C/400°F/Gas 6. Lightly grease a 23x33cm/9x13in Swiss roll tin. Cut 100g/4oz of the butter into pieces. Sift the flour into a bowl and rub in the chopped butter with your fingertips until the mixture resembles crumbs. Stir in the caster sugar and orange zest. Pour in most of the milk and mix, using a flat-bladed knife, to form a soft scone dough, adding more milk if it seems too dry.

2 Form into a ball with your hands, but don't overhandle. Roll out on a lightly floured surface to the same size as the base of the tin. Lift the dough into the tin and gently press in.

3 Scatter the plums over the scone dough and dot the remaining butter on top. Mix together the light muscovado sugar and cinnamon and sprinkle over the plums. Pour the orange juice over the top.

4 Bake for 20 minutes until the base is golden and the plums bubbling and juicy.

5 Remove from the oven, dust with icing sugar, cut into 12 squares and serve with cream or crème fraîche.

Preparation about 20 minutes
Cooking 12 minutes, plus 5
    minutes' standing

100g/4oz butter, softened, plus more
  for greasing
100g/4oz golden syrup
grated zest of 1 lemon
100g/4oz blackberries
3 ripe pears, peeled, cored and quartered
100g/4oz light muscovado sugar
100g/4oz self-raising flour
2 eggs
3 tbsp milk
cream or custard, to serve

pear and blackberry upside-down pudding

Whenever baking cake mixture in the microwave, add 2–3 tablespoons of milk to the mixture as microwaves tend to dry it out.

1 Lightly butter a 1.4 litre/2½ pint non-metallic gratin dish or a 20cm/8in microwave cake dish. Spoon the golden syrup over the base of the dish, then sprinkle over the lemon zest. Scatter over the blackberries and pears, cut side up.

2 In a large bowl, beat together the butter, sugar, flour, eggs and milk with an electric hand whisk for 2-3 minutes until light and fluffy. Spoon the mixture over the fruit and level the top.

3 Microwave on High for 12 minutes until the cake begins to come away from the sides of the dish. Allow to stand for 5 minutes, then loosen the edges and invert on to a plate. Serve warm with cream or custard.

Variation
If you don't have a microwave, preheat the oven to 180°C/375°F/Gas 4 and make the cake as for the microwave, but leave out the milk. Bake for 35-40 minutes. Allow to cool in the tin for 10 minutes before turning out.

rhubarb cheesecake pie

1 Put the orange juice in a pan with the rhubarb and 85g/3oz sugar. Cook over a low heat until the sugar dissolves, stirring, then cook for 5-8 minutes, stirring occasionally, until rhubarb is almost tender. Tip it and juice into a large sieve set over a bowl. Return juices to the pan and leave the rhubarb to cool. Set both aside.

2 Preheat the oven to 200°C/400°F/Gas 6. Make the cheesecake: beat the egg in a bowl, then beat in the soft cheese, sugar, vanilla and orange zest.

3 Make the pie: roll the pastry into a 33cm/13in circle. Trim off the corners a little to neaten the shape, but don't worry about it being too precise. Transfer to a large baking sheet. Spread the cheesecake mixture over the pastry to within about 5cm/2in of the edges. Spread the cooled rhubarb over the top, then fold the pastry edges in loose folds over the filling, leaving the centre exposed. Gently reshape the pie with your hands to make a diameter of about 23cm/9in. Mix the milk and 2 teaspoons of sugar and brush over the pastry. Bake for 30 minutes until the pastry is puffed and golden.

4 While it is baking, heat the reserved juices with the remaining sugar and boil for about 10 minutes until reduced to a thickish glaze. Drizzle half this over the rhubarb and serve the rest separately. Serve hot or warm, with whipped cream if you like.

Serves 6-8
Preparation 20 minutes
Cooking about 40 minutes

finely grated zest and juice of 1 orange
900g/2lb trimmed rhubarb, sliced
150g/5oz caster sugar
whipped cream, to serve (optional)

for the cheesecake
1 egg
400g/14oz full-fat soft cheese
50g/2oz caster sugar
½ tsp vanilla extract

for the pie
375g/13oz packet of ready-rolled puff
   pastry, defrosted if frozen
1 tsp milk
2 tsp caster sugar

greengage eggnog tart

Serves 6
Preparation 20-30 minutes
Cooking 30-40 minutes

250g/9oz ready-made shortcrust pastry,
  defrosted if frozen
flour, for dusting
900g/2lb greengages, halved and stoned
50g/2oz golden caster sugar
1 egg, beaten, for glazing
icing sugar, for sprinkling

for the eggnog custard
  150ml/¼ pint single cream
  150ml/¼ pint milk
  2 egg yolks
  1 tsp cornflour
  1 tbsp golden caster sugar
  large pinch of freshly grated nutmeg
  1 tbsp rum

This sensational tart, with a pâtisserie-style finish, is surprisingly easy to make.

1 Preheat the oven to 220°C/425°F/Gas 7 and put a flat baking sheet in the oven to heat for 15 minutes.

2 Meanwhile, roll out the pastry on a lightly floured surface to a round about 30cm/12in diameter. Put it on a baking sheet (not the one in the oven).

3 Pile the fruit into the centre, leaving a clear 2.5cm/1in edge. Sprinkle with all but a tablespoon of the sugar. Fold in the pastry edges, and loosely ruffle and pinch around the fruit.

4 Brush the pastry with beaten egg and sprinkle with the remaining caster sugar. Slip a fish slice or palette knife under the tart. Slide it on to the hot baking sheet (if you've got two implements you may find it easier to use one on each side of the tart, or you could get someone else to help you).

5 Bake for 30 minutes or until the pastry is golden brown and the greengages are tender. The juices will bubble up around the pastry as it cooks, making it slightly caramelized underneath.

6 Make the eggnog custard: stir the cream and milk together in a saucepan and bring almost to boiling point, then remove from the heat. With a wooden spoon, beat the egg yolks, cornflour and sugar in a large bowl. Pour the hot cream mixture into this custard, stirring steadily, then return the liquid to the pan and add the nutmeg. Stir over a gentle heat until thick enough to coat the back of a spoon. Remove from the heat and stir in the rum. Preheat the grill to high.

7 Remove the tart from the oven. Drizzle with 5 tablespoons of the custard. Flash under the grill for 2-3 minutes until the edges of the fruit caramelize. Sift icing sugar over the pastry edge. Serve warm with the remaining custard.

Preparation 20-30 minutes
Cooking 30-35 minutes

400g/14oz prepared rhubarb, cut into
  chunks
250g/9oz strawberries, hulled and halved
85g/3oz granulated sugar
1 tsp cornflour

for the crumble topping
100g/4oz plain flour
85g/3oz caster or light muscovado sugar
85g/3oz butter, softened
50g/2oz fine white breadcrumbs
1 tsp finely grated orange zest
¹/₂–1 tsp ground cardamom seeds
50g/2oz chopped walnuts

rhubarb, strawberry and cardamom crumble

Rhubarb and strawberries are a great American combination for pies and homely puddings. Serve warm or cold, rather than straight from the oven, for the best flavour, with thick cream, ice cream or custard.

1 Preheat the oven to 180°C/375°F/Gas 4. Mix the rhubarb chunks and the strawberries, and toss with the sugar and cornflour. Turn the mixture into a 1.2 litre/2 pint baking dish.

2 For the crumble topping, mix the flour and sugar in a bowl. Rub the butter into the flour mixture using your fingertips – the mixture should be quite lumpy. Stir in the breadcrumbs, orange zest, cardamom and walnuts.

3 Spoon the crumble mixture evenly over the fruit and bake for 30–35 minutes, or until the juices begin to bubble up through the crumble.

panettone pudding

Preparation 10 minutes
Cooking 35 minutes

50g/2oz butter, softened
250g/9oz panettone (about 5 medium slices)
2 eggs
142ml/¼ pint carton of double cream
225ml/8fl oz milk
1 tsp vanilla extract
2 tbsp caster sugar
icing sugar, for sprinkling
softly whipped cream, to serve

Panettone, the fluffy Italian cross between bread and cake, is a popular gift at Christmas. If you find yourself with more than you need after the festivities, try this posh version of bread and butter pudding.

1 Preheat the oven to 160°C/325°F/Gas 3 and grease a 850ml/1½ pint shallow baking dish with a little butter. Cut the panettone into wedges, leaving the crusts on. Butter the slices lightly with the rest of the butter. Cut the slices in half and arrange them in the dish, buttered side up.

2 In a bowl, whisk together the eggs, cream, milk, vanilla extract and caster sugar, and pour evenly over the panettone.

3 Put the dish in a roasting tin and pour hot water around it to a depth of about 2.5cm/1in. Bake for 35 minutes until the pudding is just set – it should be yellow inside and nicely browned on top. Dust with icing sugar and serve with spoonfuls of whipped cream.

rippled chocolate bombe

Cuts into 12 slices
Preparation 45 minutes, plus
cooling
Cooking 1½ hours–1 hour 40
minutes

250g/9oz butter, softened, plus more for
greasing
150g/5oz bar of good-quality plain
chocolate (at least 70% cocoa solids)
225g/8oz golden caster sugar
4 large eggs
225g/8oz plain flour
2 tsp baking powder
100g/4oz ground almonds
3 tbsp cocoa powder
1 tbsp milk
2 tsp vanilla extract
candied fruits or candied orange strips, to
decorate
crème fraîche, to serve

for the chocolate cream
142ml/¼ pint carton of double cream
175g/6oz good-quality plain chocolate (at
least 70% cocoa solids), broken into
pieces

If you want a dessert to impress your dinner guests, this is it. Apart from its stunning good looks, it has an added wow factor when you cut into it. But whatever you do, don't tell anyone how easy the marbling is!

1 Preheat the oven to 160°C/325°F/Gas 3. Grease a 1.7 litre/3 pint stainless-steel mixing bowl and line the base (approximately 9cm/3½in) with a circle of greaseproof paper.

2 Break the chocolate into pieces in a heatproof bowl. Add 25g/1oz of the butter and stand the bowl over a pan of gently simmering water until the chocolate has melted (or melt it in the microwave). Stir until smooth.

3 Put the remaining butter in a separate bowl with the sugar, eggs, flour, baking powder and 85g/3oz of the almonds. Beat together for 2–3 minutes until smooth and creamy. Spoon 350g/12oz of this mixture into another bowl and stir in the cocoa powder and milk. Stir the remaining almonds and the vanilla extract into the remaining plain cake mixture.

4 Spread a little of the vanilla mixture in the base of the bowl. Top with a spoonful of the cocoa mixture, then a little of the chocolate sauce, taking care not to let the chocolate sauce get near the edge of the bowl or it will burn during baking. Continue to alternate the three mixtures in the bowl, placing large spoonfuls in at random and spreading them slightly to mix up the colours. Level the surface, then swirl a skewer or the end of a teaspoon through the mixture, a few times, to ripple the colours together. Don't overmix or the colours will lose their definition.

5 Bake for 1 hour 30 minutes to 1 hour 40 minutes, until the cake is risen and the surface feels firm to the touch. To check that the cake is done, pierce the light part of the cake with a skewer - it should come out clean. Leave to cool in the bowl, then loosen the edges and invert the cake on to a flat serving plate.

6 Make the chocolate cream: heat the cream in a small heavy-based saucepan until hot and beginning to bubble round the edges. Add the chocolate pieces and remove from the heat, stirring gently. Pour into a bowl and leave until the chocolate has melted. Chill for about 30 minutes, stirring occasionally, until the mixture just holds its shape when beaten.

7 Using a palette knife, swirl the chocolate cream over the top and sides of the cake. Slice the candied fruits and use to decorate the top of the cake. Keep in a cool place (not the fridge) until ready to serve. This is a luxurious dessert, so serve thin slivers with a dollop of crème fraîche to cut through the richness.

Serves 10
Preparation 1–1¼ hours, plus
freezing and cooling

225g/8oz good-quality dark chocolate
(50–70% cocoa solids)
150g/5oz unsalted butter, cubed and
softened
150g/5oz golden caster sugar
25g/1oz good-quality cocoa powder
284ml/½ pint carton of double cream
whites of 3 medium free-range eggs
250ml/9fl oz cherry liqueur or brandy
275g/10oz cherries, fresh or canned
(about three cans, drained), pitted
500g /1lb 2oz tub of mascarpone cheese

cherry chocolate terrine

1 Melt the chocolate and half the butter in a bowl over a pan of gently simmering water (or in the microwave on Medium for 3 minutes). When melted, stir with a wooden spoon until you have a smooth consistency, then allow to cool slightly.

2 Line a 1.73-litre/3-pint loaf tin with cling film. In a large bowl, beat the rest the butter with two-thirds of the sugar until smooth. Stir in the cocoa until you have a smooth chocolatey paste. Whisk the cream to soft peaks but no further. Wash the beaters, then whisk the egg whites to soft peaks. Stir in 125ml/4fl oz of the cherry liqueur or brandy and the cooled melted chocolate and butter into the cocoa butter paste. Stir in the cherries, then fold in the whipped cream, followed by the egg whites. Pour into the terrine, gently bang on a hard surface to settle and freeze until solid.

3 Pour the remaining cherry brandy and sugar into a small heavy-based saucepan and bring to the boil. Reduce by two-thirds to make a syrup, then allow to cool.

4 Take terrine from freezer and tip out. Line tin with fresh cling film. As soon as terrine is soft enough to slice but still firm, 10-15 minutes, slice with a sharp knife. Return slices to tin, interleaved with greaseproof paper. Cover and return to freezer.

5 One hour before serving, transfer to the fridge. Just before serving, lay a slice of the terrine on a spoonful of mascarpone, then drizzle each plate with syrup.

mars bar mousses

Most chocolate mousses are made with bitter dark chocolate and they're not always popular with children, but these are made with Mars bars so they taste mild and fudgy and everyone loves them. In the photograph, they've been dressed up for a dinner party, but for a family pud you can set the mixture in one large bowl for everyone to dive into. Please note that both this and the recipe opposite contain raw eggs and should be avoided by the very young, the elderly and pregnant women.

1 Put the Mars bars, milk and cocoa in a heavy-based saucepan. Cook over a very gentle heat, stirring constantly, until the chocolate has melted. Transfer to a bowl and leave to cool for 15 minutes, whisking frequently with a wire whisk to blend in any pieces of fudge that rise to the surface, leaving a smooth mixture.

2 Whisk the egg whites in a separate bowl until peaking softly. Using a metal spoon, fold a quarter of the whites into the chocolate sauce to lighten it, then fold in the remainder.

3 Turn the mixture into 6 small cups, glasses or ramekins and chill in the fridge to set, for at least 2 hours, before serving. Serve topped with chocolate shavings.

Serves 6
Preparation 15-20 minutes, plus setting
Cooking 2-3 minutes

4 standard (65g) Mars bars, chopped into pieces
3 tbsp milk
4 tbsp cocoa powder
whites of 3 large eggs
chocolate shavings, to decorate

**Serves 6 (16–17 crêpes, 2–3 per
person)**
Preparation 10-12 minutes
Cooking about 20 minutes

100g/4oz plain flour
1 tbsp golden caster sugar
pinch of salt
2 large eggs
1 tbsp sunflower oil, plus more for greasing
300ml/¹⁄₂ pint semi-skimmed milk
splash of beer, about 2 tbsp (optional)

for the sauce
100g/4oz butter
100g/4oz golden caster sugar
150ml/¹⁄₄ pint freshly squeezed orange
*   juice (about 2 large oranges)*
2 tsp finely grated orange zest
1 tsp finely grated lemon zest
3 tbsp Grand Marnier
2 tbsp cognac

crêpes suzette

1 Put the flour, sugar and salt in a large bowl. Make a well in the centre, add the eggs, oil and 2 tablespoons of milk, and beat together until smooth. Slowly start to pour in a little milk, mixing as you pour, to keep batter smooth. Pour in the rest of the milk, a bit more quickly now, until it looks like single cream. Add the beer.

2 Heat a 15cm/6in crêpe pan wiped with oiled kitchen paper. Pour 2¹⁄₂ tablespoons of batter into the pan, moving it around so the batter fits the bottom. When golden underneath (about 15 seconds if at right temperature), turn and cook for 30 seconds, until spotted brown. Slide on to a plate. Wipe pan again with oiled kitchen paper and continue until all the batter is used, stacking the crêpes on top of each other.

3 For the sauce, heat the butter and sugar in a deep frying pan over a low heat, stirring occasionally, until the sugar begins to dissolve; turn up the heat and bubble quite fast, until the mixture just starts to go brown and caramelize (about 4 minutes), stirring only towards the end. Pour in the orange juice, then add the orange and lemon zest, and allow to bubble for 3-4 minutes to thicken slightly. Add the Grand Marnier and cognac, heat for a few seconds and then lower the heat.

4 Put a crêpe into the juices and, holding it with a fork, coat it well in the mixture. Fold it into quarters and push to one side of the pan. Continue the coating and folding with the remaining pancakes. Serve 2-3 crêpes per person with the sauce.

butterscotch apple charlotte

1 First make the butterscotch sauce: melt the butter in a small pan. Stir in sugar and cook over low heat, stirring, until dissolved. Pour in the cream. Increase heat and boil for about 2 minutes, whisking until slightly thickened and glossy. Leave to cool.

2 Put the apples in a large pan and stir in the lemon zest and juice. Cover and cook on a very low heat for 8–10 minutes, until tender. Preheat oven to 190°C/375°F/Gas 5.

3 Use a little butter to brush inside of a round 23x6cm/9x2½in springform tin lightly. Butter both sides of each bread slice. Mix the sugar and cinnamon, and sprinkle over 1 side of each buttered slice. Lay 2 whole slices (sugar down) in base of tin. Cut the rest in half. Use 2 to fill spaces in the base, cutting to fit. Set aside 6 halves. Arrange rest, upright and overlapping against side of tin, with sugar facing out. Don't leave gaps.

4 Beat egg in a bowl and stir in one-third of sauce. Add apples and spoon into bread case. Sprinkle over two-thirds of pecans, then pour in half remaining sauce. Cover with reserved bread (sugar up), cutting to fit. Gently fold tips in towards middle. Press to ensure it lies flat. Slide on baking sheet and bake for 30 minutes. Scatter rest of pecans on top and return to oven for 5 minutes until golden. Remove and let stand for 10 minutes. Remove tin, dust with icing sugar and serve with crème fraîche and rest of sauce.

Serves 8
Preparation 45 minutes
Cooking time 35 minutes

1.3kg/3lb cooking apples, peeled, cored and cut into thick slices
finely grated zest and juice of 1 large lemon
150g/5oz butter, melted
1 large unsliced white tin loaf, preferably a day old to make slicing and fitting easier, crusts removed and cut into thin slices
25g/1oz golden caster sugar
½ tsp ground cinnamon
1 egg
85g/3oz pecan halves, roughly chopped
200g/7oz tub of crème fraîche, to serve

for the butterscotch sauce
85g/3oz butter
100g/4oz light muscovado sugar
200ml/7fl oz double cream

low-fat puds

Enjoying a truly scrummy pud needn't automatically mean abandoning your diet. Judicious use of low-fat Greek-style yoghurt instead of cream and cutting back sugar quantities not only reduce the calories, but sometimes even improve the result, producing more temptingly complex flavours.

strawberry and banana knickerbocker glories

Knickerbocker glories are spectacular and colourful. Here we use yoghurt instead of cream for a lighter texture, and a deliciously smooth purée of strawberry and banana swirls through the different layers. The main thing is to use your tallest dessert glasses, to show off the layers.

Preparation 15 minutes

450g/1lb strawberries, hulled
2 bananas
1 tbsp caster sugar, plus 1 tsp
500ml/18fl oz carton of low-fat Greek-style yoghurt
4 scoops of vanilla ice cream, preferably reduced-fat, to serve
25g/1oz whole toasted hazelnuts, very roughly chopped

1 Purée one-third of the strawberries with half a banana and 1 tablespoon of caster sugar until smooth.
2 Slice and roughly chop the remaining strawberries. Slice the rest of the bananas and mix together with the chopped strawberries and the teaspoon of caster sugar. Stir the yogurt until smooth.
3 Now start layering. Spoon a little of the yoghurt into the bottom of 4 tall glasses, then layer up with the fruit and a drizzle of purée. Repeat the layers, finishing with yoghurt.
4 Top with a scoop of ice cream, drizzle over a little purée and finish with a sprinkling of hazelnuts.

rhubarb and ginger pavlova

Serves 8
Preparation 1 hour–1 hour 15 minutes, plus 1 hour cooling
Cooking 1 hour 25 minutes

2 tsp cornflour
1 tsp white wine vinegar
1 tsp vanilla extract
whites of 5 eggs
200g/7oz caster sugar

for the topping
450g/1lb prepared rhubarb, cut into 2.5cm/1in lengths
2 pieces of preserved stem ginger in syrup, finely chopped, plus 2 tbsp of the syrup
about 85g/3oz caster sugar
450ml/¾ pint low-fat Greek-style yoghurt
finely grated zest of 1 lime

1 Preheat the oven to 130°C/275°F/Gas 1. Line a large baking sheet with non-stick baking paper and draw a 23cm/9in circle on it. Stir the cornflour, vinegar and vanilla together.
2 Whisk the egg whites until stiff. Whisk in the cornflour mixture and sugar, a little at a time, until glossy and stiff. Spoon into the circle, making a slight indentation in the centre. Bake for 1 hour. Turn off the oven and leave pavlova in it until cold. Peel off paper and set aside.
3 When the pavlova base is cold, prepare the topping: preheat the oven to 190°C/375°F/Gas 5. Put the rhubarb, ginger syrup, sugar and 2 tablespoons of water in an ovenproof

dish. Bake for 15 minutes until rhubarb is tender but still whole. Allow to cool, add more sugar to taste and drain the juices into a pan. Boil rapidly for 5 minutes until syrupy. Set aside.

4 Whisk the yoghurt until it just holds its shape. Fold in the chopped ginger and lime zest. Heap into the centre of the pavlova. Top with rhubarb just before serving. Spoon over a little syrup and serve the rest in a jug.

mango and passion fruit roulade

Serves 6
Preparation 30 minutes
Cooking time 30 minutes

whites of 3 large eggs
175g/6oz caster sugar
1 level tsp cornflour
1 tsp malt vinegar
1 tsp vanilla extract
225g/8oz low-fat Greek-style yoghurt
1 large ripe mango, peeled and diced
pulp from 4 passion fruit
icing sugar and physalis fruits, to decorate

for the quick raspberry sauce
225g/8oz frozen raspberries, defrosted
2 tbsp icing sugar

1 Preheat the oven to 150°C/300°F/ Gas 2. Line a 33x23cm/13x9in Swiss roll tin with non-stick baking parchment.

2 Beat the egg whites with an electric whisk until frothy and doubled in bulk. Slowly whisk in the sugar until thick and shiny. Whisk in the cornflour, vinegar and vanilla extract.

3 Spoon into the prepared tin and gently level. Bake for 30 minutes or until the surface is just firm.

4 Dust some baking parchment with icing sugar. Remove the meringue from the oven. Cover with damp greaseproof paper for 10 minutes then remove. Turn out on to the parchment and peel off the lining paper.

5 While the meringue is standing, make the raspberry sauce: process the raspberries in a blender until sauce-like and pulse in the icing sugar. Press through a sieve.

6 Spread the yoghurt on the meringue, then scatter with mango and passion fruit. Use the parchment to help roll up the sheet of meringue from one short end. Decorate with icing sugar and physalis, and serve with the raspberry sauce.

strawberry and cinnamon torte

Serves 6-8
Preparation 15 minutes
Cooking about 1 hour

175g/6oz butter, softened, plus more for greasing
175g/6oz ground almonds
175g/6oz golden caster sugar
175g/6oz self-raising flour
1 tsp ground cinnamon
1 egg, plus 1 extra yolk
450g/1lb strawberries, hulled and sliced
icing sugar, for dusting
whipped double cream mixed with Greek-style yoghurt, to serve

This crumbly dessert is perfect for a summer Sunday lunch or dinner and is just as good made with raspberries.

1 Preheat the oven to 180°C/350°F/Gas 4. Line the base of a loose-bottomed 23cm/9in cake tin with greaseproof paper and grease the sides.

2 In a food processor, combine the butter, ground almonds, sugar, flour, cinnamon, egg and extra yolk until evenly mixed.

3 Spread half the mixture over the base of the tin in a smooth layer with no gaps – it's easiest to do this with two forks. Put the strawberries on top. Top with the remaining cake mixture and spread smooth.

4 Bake for about 1 hour. Check after 40 minutes – if the torte is getting too brown, cover loosely with foil. When cooked, the torte should be slightly risen and dark golden brown.

5 Allow to cool slightly in the tin, then loosen the edges with a knife and remove from the tin. Slide on to a plate and dust with icing sugar. Serve warm, in wedges, with spoonfuls of cream and Greek yoghurt.

cinnamon, raisin and orange rice pudding

Serves 6-8
Preparation 10 minutes
Cooking 1½ hours

85g/3oz short-grain pudding rice
85g/3oz caster sugar
25g/1oz butter
1.25 litres/2 pints full-fat milk
½ tsp ground cinnamon
85g/3oz raisins
grated zest of 1 orange
freshly grated nutmeg

1 Put all the ingredients except the nutmeg in a large pan. Bring slowly to the boil, stir, then simmer, uncovered, for 30 minutes, stirring occasionally.

2 Preheat the oven to 150°C/300°F/Gas 2. Butter a 1.7 litre/3 pint ovenproof dish and pour in the rice pudding mixture. Sprinkle the top with freshly grated nutmeg and bake for 1 hour until the rice is tender and a golden-brown skin has formed.

3 Leave to cool for 10 minutes before serving as the rice will be very hot.

Buoying bakes

PERHAPS THE MOST COMFORTING OF FOODS ARE THOSE

LITTLE SWEET SNACKS THROUGHOUT THE DAY THAT

ACCOMPANY CUPS OF TEA OR COFFEE, BE THEY

BISCUITS, COOKIES, PIECES OF CAKE, OR EVEN SLICES

OF COUNTRY-STYLE BREAD THICK WITH BUTTER

AND JAM, THEY CAN SOMETIMES BE THE HIGHLIGHT

OF OUR DAY.

mocha truffle roulade

Serves 8
Preparation 30 minutes
Cooking 20-25 minutes

butter, for greasing
4 eggs, separated
100g/4oz caster sugar
150g/5oz walnuts, finely chopped
25g/1oz cocoa powder
4 tbsp fine white or brown breadcrumbs
2 tbsp very strong black coffee
1/2 tsp vanilla extract
icing sugar, for sprinkling and dusting

for the filling
1 tbsp rum or Tia Maria
2 tbsp very strong black coffee
284ml/1/2 pint carton of double cream
85g/3oz chocolate truffles, chopped

1 Preheat the oven to 180°C/350°F/Gas 4. Lightly butter a Swiss roll tin about 35x25cm/14x10in and line with non-stick baking parchment.

2 Whisk the egg yolks and sugar together until very pale. Mix the nuts, cocoa and breadcrumbs, and fold into the egg yolk mixture. Stir in the coffee and vanilla.

3 In a clean bowl, whisk the egg whites until stiff, then fold into the mixture. Pour into the tin, level and bake for 20-25 minutes, or until just firm in the centre. Allow to cool in the tin for 5 minutes.

4 Sprinkle the icing sugar over a sheet of baking parchment and turn the cake out on it. Cover with a damp tea towel and leave to cool completely.

5 Make the filling: stir the rum or Tia Maria into the coffee and then stir that into the cream. Whisk gently until stiff. Spread over the cake and press the truffles in gently. Using the paper to help roll the cake up from one short end into a roulade. Transfer to a plate and dust with icing sugar to serve.

dark chocolate and orange cake

Cuts into 10 slices
Preparation 40 minutes
Cooking 1 1/2 hours, plus cooling

1 Seville orange
a little melted butter, for greasing
100g/4oz plain chocolate, broken into
  pieces
3 eggs
275g/10oz caster sugar
240ml/8 1/2 fl oz sunflower oil
25g/1oz cocoa powder
250g/9oz plain flour
1 1/2 tsp baking powder
candied orange peel, to decorate

for the chocolate ganache
225g/8oz plain chocolate, broken into
  pieces
225ml/8fl oz double cream

1 Pierce the orange with a skewer (right through). Cook in boiling water for 30 minutes until soft. Whiz the whole orange in a food processor until smooth; let cool.

2 Preheat the oven to 180°C/350°F/Gas 4. Grease and line the base of a 23cm/9in round cake tin. Melt the chocolate in a heatproof bowl set over a pan of simmering water or in the microwave for 2 minutes on High, stirring after 1 minute. Let cool.

3 In a large bowl, lightly beat the eggs, sugar and oil. Gradually beat in the puréed orange, discarding any pips, then stir in the cooled melted chocolate. Sift in the cocoa, flour and baking powder. Mix well and pour into the tin. Bake in the centre of the oven for 55 minutes, or until the cake springs back when lightly pressed in the middle. (Check after 45 minutes and cover with foil if it is browning too much.) Allow to cool for 10 minutes in the tin, then turn out on to a wire rack to cool completely.

4 Make the chocolate ganache: put the chocolate into a heatproof bowl. Bring the cream to the boil and pour over the chocolate. Leave for 2 minutes, then stir until smooth. Set aside until firm enough to spread over the cake - up to 1 1/2 hours.

5 Transfer the cake to a serving plate. Using a palette knife, swirl the ganache over the top. Decorate with strips of candied orange peel.

Serves 8
Preparation 25–35 minutes, plus
**   soaking**
Cooking about 30 minutes

250g/9oz no-soak prunes, halved
4 tbsp brandy
50g/2oz butter, plus more for greasing
25g/1oz cocoa powder
100g/4oz plain chocolate (at least 70%
*   cocoa solids), broken into pieces*
175g/6oz golden caster sugar
100ml/3½fl oz hot water
whites of 4 large eggs
85g/3oz plain flour
1 tsp ground cinnamon
lightly whipped cream or crème fraîche,
*   to serve*

prune and chocolate torte

Rich with brandy-steeped prunes, this is a cake for real lovers of chocolate. The very best way to serve it is slightly warm, with lavish spoonfuls of lightly whipped cream or crème fraîche.

1 Put the prunes and brandy in a small bowl and leave to steep about 30 minutes, until most of brandy has been absorbed.

2 Preheat the oven to 190°C/375°F/Gas 5. Grease a 23cm/9in loose-bottomed cake tin or springform pan. Put the butter, cocoa, chocolate and 150g/5oz of the sugar in a pan, add the hot water and gently heat until mixture is smooth. Leave to cool slightly.

3 Whisk the egg whites to soft peaks, then gradually whisk in the remaining sugar. Sift the flour and cinnamon over and gently fold in with a metal spoon, until almost combined. Add the chocolate mix and fold in until evenly combined.

4 Pour the mixture into the tin and arrange the prunes over the top (they will sink into the sponge during baking). Sprinkle over any remaining brandy and bake for about 30 minutes until just firm. Serve with cream or crème fraîche.

toffee brownies

Cuts into 16 squares
Preparation 20-30 minutes
Cooking 30-35 minutes

225g/8oz unsalted butter, in pieces, plus
more for greasing
300g/10oz dark chocolate (preferably
around 50–60% cocoa solids), broken
into pieces
3 large eggs
225g/8oz dark muscovado sugar
100g/4oz plain flour
1 tsp baking powder
1 or 2 drops of vanilla extract

1 Preheat the oven to 160°C/325°F/Gas 3 and butter and line the base of a shallow 23cm/9in square cake tin.

2 Melt the butter and chocolate together (you can do this in the microwave, it takes about 2 minutes), then stir well and cool slightly.

3 Beat the eggs until pale, then whisk in the sugar until thick and glossy and well combined. Gently fold in the melted chocolate mixture, then sift in the flour and baking powder, and add the vanilla extract. Stir gently until smooth.

4 Pour into the prepared cake tin and bake for 30–35 minutes, or until firm to the touch. Test by inserting a wooden cocktail stick into the middle – there should be a few moist crumbs sticking to it. The mixture will still be soft in the centre, but will firm up on cooling.

5 Allow to cool in the tin on a wire rack for at least 1 hour – if you can resist the temptation to eat them – then cut into 16 squares and allow to cool completely on the rack.

mango, banana and coconut cake

Cuts into 10 slices
Preparation 20 minutes
Cooking 30-35 minutes

225g/8oz butter, softened, plus extra for
greasing
1 medium ripe mango, peeled and stoned
1 tsp vanilla essence
2 ripe bananas, mashed
150g/5oz light muscovado sugar
2 eggs, beaten
50g/2oz desiccated coconut
225g/8oz self-raising flour
1/2 tsp bicarbonate of soda
1 tsp mixed spice

for the filling
200g/7oz full-fat soft cheese
2 tsp lemon juice
25g/1oz icing sugar, plus extra for dusting

1 Preheat the oven to 160°C/325°F/Gas 3. Butter and line the bases of 2 round 20cm/8in sandwich tins with greaseproof paper. Chop the mango then purée in a food processor. Mix half the mango purée and the vanilla into the bananas.

2 In a bowl, beat the butter and sugar until light and fluffy. Beat in the eggs, a little at a time, then stir in the mango mixture and the coconut – don't worry if it looks curdled. Sift in the flour, bicarbonate of soda and mixed spice, then fold in lightly until just mixed.

3 Divide the mixture between the tins and smooth the tops. Bake for 30-35 minutes until risen and firm to the touch. Allow to cool in the tins for 5 minutes, then turn out on to a wire rack, peel off the paper and leave to cool completely.

4 Make the filling: beat together the cheese, lemon juice and sugar, then stir in the reserved mango. Spread one cake with filling, put the other on top and dust lightly with icing sugar.

ginger and lemon sponge

Cuts into 8 slices
Preparation 30 minutes, plus cooling
Cooking 25 minutes

100g/4oz soft margarine
100g/4oz caster sugar
2 eggs
100g/4oz golden syrup
225g/8oz self-raising flour
2 tsp ground ginger
pinch of grated nutmeg
2 tbsp milk

for the filling
50g/2oz butter, softened
175g/6oz icing sugar, sifted
2 tbsp lemon curd

for the icing
175g/6oz icing sugar, sifted
finely grated zest of 1 lemon and 1 tbsp juice

1 Preheat the oven to 160°C/325°F/Gas 3. Grease 2 deep 20cm/8in sandwich cake tins and line the base of each with greaseproof paper.

2 Beat the margarine and sugar until fluffy. Beat in the eggs and golden syrup. Sift the flour, ginger and nutmeg together. Pour the milk into the margarine mixture and tip into the flour mixture. Fold until blended.

3 Divide the mix between the tins and bake for 25 minutes until the centre of each springs back when lightly pressed. Leave in the tins for 5 minutes, then turn out on to a wire rack. Peel off the lining papers and leave the cakes until cold.

4 Make the filling: beat the butter until creamy, add the icing sugar and lemon curd. Mix and spread over one of the cakes, then sandwich them together.

5 Make the icing: mix the icing sugar with the lemon zest, juice and 3-4 teaspoons hot water until smooth. Spread over the cake with a palette knife and leave to set.

Cuts into 10 slices
Preparation 30-40 minutes
Cooking 50 minutes

150g/5oz butter, softened, plus more for
greasing
225g/8oz plums
2 eggs, plus 1 extra yolk
pinch of salt
150g/5oz golden caster sugar
150g/5oz self-raising flour
grated zest and juice of 1 orange

for the topping
1¹/₂ tbsp fresh lemon juice
225g/8oz golden caster sugar
25g/1oz rough sugar pieces, roughly
crushed

autumn plum crunch cake

1 Preheat the oven to 160°C/325°F/Gas 3. Grease a 1.25 litre/2 pint loaf tin and line the base. Halve and stone the plums, then roughly chop half of them and cut the rest into wedges. Lightly beat the eggs and extra yolk with the pinch of salt.

2 Beat the butter and sugar in a bowl until light and fluffy. Pour in the eggs a little at a time, beating well after each addition. Fold in the flour with the orange zest and 2 tablespoons of the juice, then fold in the chopped plums. Spoon the mixture into the prepared tin and scatter the plum wedges here and there over the top. Bake for about 50 minutes or until a skewer inserted into the centre of the cake comes out clean.

3 Remove the cake from the oven. Leave in the tin for 10 minutes, then turn out and stand the right way up on a wire rack set over a baking sheet with raised sides.

4 For the topping, mix the remaining orange juice with the lemon juice and caster sugar. Spoon on top of the cooling cake and sprinkle with the crushed sugar pieces. Set aside for about 1 hour, or until the sugar sets into a rough icing.

cherry and almond cake

Cuts into 12 slices
Preparation 15-20 minutes
Cooking 1 hour 10 minutes

200g/7oz softened butter, plus more for greasing
100g/4oz blanched almonds
225g/8oz golden caster sugar
3 eggs
200g/7oz self-raising flour
250g/9oz glacé cherries, halved
50g/2oz flaked almonds

1 Preheat the oven to 180°C/350°F/Gas 4. Butter the base and sides of a deep 20cm/8in cake tin, then line the base with a circle of baking parchment.

2 Put the blanched almonds in a baking tray in one layer and toast in the oven for 7-8 minutes until just golden. Tip into a food processor and whiz until finely ground. (Don't overwork or they'll release too much of their oil into the cake.)

3 Put the butter and sugar in a large bowl and beat together until pale and fluffy, about 5 minutes. Add the eggs one at a time with a little of the flour, beating well between each addition. (Adding a little of the flour helps to stop the mix curdling.) Fold in the almonds and remaining flour. Use a large metal spoon for this, taking care not to knock out too much air. Gently stir in the halved cherries until evenly distributed. Spoon mixture into the tin and smooth top with a palette knife or the back of a metal spoon. This helps give an even rise. Cover with the flaked almonds.

4 Bake the cake in the centre of the oven for 1 hour 10 minutes. (Don't open the oven door for the first hour or the cake may sink.) To check if the cake is cooked, insert a fine skewer into the centre – it should come out clean.

5 Remove the cake from the tin and let it cool completely on a rack before slicing.

pastis

This classic pastry from southwest France is traditionally made from a paper-thin strudel-like dough 'as thin as a bride's veil'. Here filo pastry is used.

Serves 6
Preparation 40 minutes, plus 2 hours' soaking
Cooking 30-35 minutes

20 prunes (about 225g/8oz)
4 tbsp Armagnac
3 tbsp tea
6 eating apples, peeled and thickly sliced
85g/3oz butter, plus more for greasing
6 tbsp caster sugar
grated zest of 1 lemon
6 sheets (about 28x37cm/11x14³/₄in) of filo pastry, defrosted if frozen
2 digestive biscuits, crumbled
icing sugar, for sifting

1 Soak the prunes in the Armagnac and tea for about 2 hours.

2 Cook the apples gently in 25g/1oz of the butter with half the sugar and the lemon zest for 5 minutes. Add the prunes and marinade, and take off the heat.

3 Preheat the oven to 220°C/425°F/Gas 7 and butter a large baking sheet. Melt the remaining butter. Take one sheet of filo (keep the others covered with a damp tea towel), brush with melted butter and place on the baking tray. Repeat with the others, overlapping them at an angle to look like the petals of a flower. Sprinkle a circle of biscuit crumbs over the top, halfway in from the edges, to keep the filo crisp. Spread the apples, prunes and juices on top, then either gather the ends and twist like a bundle, or crumple gently with your fingers to make a ruffled top. Brush with a little melted butter and dust with the remaining caster sugar.

4 Bake for 10 minutes, lower the oven to 180°C/350°F/Gas 4 and bake for 15-20 minutes more, until brown and crisp. Serve, sifted with icing sugar.

Battenberg cake

Cuts into 8 slices
Preparation 50 minutes
Cooking 30 minutes

100g/4oz butter, at room temperature, plus more for greasing
100g/4oz caster sugar, plus more for sprinkling
100g/4oz self-raising flour
1 tsp baking powder
2 eggs
a few drops of red food colouring
4 tbsp raspberry jam, warmed and sieved
3 tbsp apricot jam, warmed and sieved

for the almond paste
100g/4oz caster sugar
100g/4oz icing sugar
100g/4oz ground almonds
2 egg yolks, plus a little egg white
a few drops of almond essence

1 Preheat the oven to 180°C/350°F/Gas 4, butter a 18cm/7in square cake tin and line the base. Cover a cardboard oblong with foil and fit down the centre of the tin. Put the butter and sugar in a bowl. Sift over the flour and baking powder and drop in the eggs. Beat with a hand blender until combined, then beat again for 1 minute.

2 Divide the mixture in half. Stir the red colouring into one half until evenly pink. Spoon plain cake mix into one half of tin and the pink into the other, smoothing the surfaces. Bake for 30 minutes until firm. Turn out, remove divider and let cool.

3 Make the paste: in a bowl, mix together the sugars and almonds. Stir in the egg yolks and almond essence, adding a little egg white to make a stiff paste. Knead briefly until the mixture comes together. Wrap in plastic film until needed.

4 Cut each half cake in half lengthwise to make 4 oblongs. Trim straight with no crisp edges. Stack together with raspberry jam to form a chequered pattern. On a large sheet of greaseproof paper sprinkled with caster sugar, roll out paste so it is long and wide enough to cover the 4 sides, then brush with apricot jam. Put cake in the middle and press paste round it so the join meets in the middle. Turn over and gently pinch paste along the 2 top edges between thumb and first finger. Thinly slice off each end to neaten, lightly score a diamond pattern on top and sprinkle with sugar.

Cuts into 12 slices
Preparation 20 minutes
Cooking about 40 minutes, plus 2
**   hours' rising**

for the first stage of the dough
100g/4oz strong white bread flour
7g/¹/₄oz sachet of easy-blend yeast
1 tsp light muscovado sugar
250ml/9fl oz lukewarm milk

for the dough
350g/12oz strong white bread flour
¹/₂ tsp salt
50g/2oz butter, plus more for greasing
1 level tbsp mixed spice
50g/2oz light muscovado sugar
225g/8oz best-quality mixed dried fruit
1 egg, beaten
oil, for greasing

for the crosses and glaze
2 tbsp plain flour
1 tsp milk
2 tsp caster sugar

hot cross bun loaf

1 For the first stage: in a large bowl, mix the flour, yeast and sugar, then slowly beat in the milk to make a smooth batter. Cover with film and leave for about 20 minutes until frothy. This is known as a 'yeast batter' and helps make the loaf softer and lighter.

2 Make the dough: put the flour and salt in a bowl and rub in butter. Stir in the spice, sugar and fruit. Add the egg to the yeast batter, then add flour mixture. Mix to a soft dough. Tip on to a lightly floured surface and knead for 8-10 minutes until smooth and not sticky, dusting the surface with a little flour. Put in a lightly buttered bowl, cover with film and leave in a warm place for 45-60 minutes, until doubled in size.

3 Butter a 900g/2lb loaf tin. Knead dough to knock out air. Cut into 3 equal pieces and shape each into an oval the width of the tin and a third its length. Place in tin and put in a large oiled food bag, allowing space for rising. Leave for about 45 minutes until risen to about 2.5cm/1in above top of tin. Preheat oven to 200°C/400°F/Gas 6.

4 Make crosses: mix flour with 5 teaspoons water to a smooth paste. Spoon into a small piping bag. Pipe 3 crosses over top of loaf. Bake for 20 minutes, loosely cover with foil and bake for 15-20 minutes more. Remove from tin and tap bottom – it sounds hollow if cooked. If not, return to tin and bake for 5 minutes, then test again. Remove from tin and cool on a rack. Make the glaze: mix the milk and sugar, and brush over the hot loaf. Leave to cool before serving, cut into slices and buttered.

comfort cottage loaf

1 Put the flour in a large bowl. Cut the butter into pieces and rub into the flour between your fingers until it resembles fine crumbs. Stir in the yeast, salt and sugar.

2 In a small pan, heat the milk until lukewarm, then gradually pour into the flour mixture, mixing to a soft dough. Put the dough on a lightly floured surface and knead for 10 minutes. Transfer to a large oiled bowl, cover with a tea towel or plastic film and leave in a warm place for 45 minutes–1 hour, until doubled in size.

3 Remove the dough from the bowl and punch it back to knock out air. Cut off a quarter and shape both pieces into rounds. Place the larger on a greased baking sheet with the smaller on top. Press together lightly. Dip a floured wooden spoon handle through the centre of both balls of dough until it touches the baking sheet.

4 Cover the loaf loosely with oiled plastic film or a clean tea towel and leave to rise for about 30 minutes until doubled in size. (The timing will depend on the warmth of your kitchen.) Preheat the oven to 200°C/400°F/Gas 6.

5 Brush the loaf all over with beaten egg, then bake in the centre of the oven for 30 minutes until golden. Tap the base of the loaf with your fingers. If it sounds hollow it is done. Set aside to cool on a wire rack.

Makes 1 loaf
Preparation 15 minutes, plus about
  1½ hours' rising time
Cooking 30 minutes

600g/1lb 5 oz strong white unbleached
  bread flour, plus more for sprinkling
50g/2oz butter, at room temperature
7g/¼oz sachet of easy-blend yeast
1 tsp salt
2 tsp caster sugar
400ml/14fl oz full-fat milk
oil, for greasing
beaten egg, to glaze

cheering cookies

Yes, bought biscuits and cookies are probably the most usual type of instant comfort food, but the sheer joy of making your own and tucking into them while they are still warm from the oven takes a lot of beating. As these recipes show, they can also be quite amazingly sophisticated.

chocolate salami

Makes about 25 slices
Preparation 20 minutes, plus chilling

250g/9oz plain chocolate
100g/4oz butter
3 tbsp clear honey
100g/4oz ground almonds
100g/4oz dried apricots, finely chopped
50g/2oz toasted chopped nuts
225g/8oz amaretti biscuits, finely crushed

1 Break up the chocolate and cut the butter into cubes. Put the chocolate, butter and honey in a large bowl. Microwave on Medium for 3-4 minutes, then stir until the mixture is smooth and glossy. (You can also melt the chocolate by setting the bowl over a pan of hot water.)
2 Stir the ground almonds, dried apricots, chopped nuts and three-quarters of the biscuits into the chocolate mixture. Leave to cool, then chill for 1-2 hours until the mixture is firm enough to shape.
3 Spoon the chocolate mixture along the length of a sheet of greaseproof

paper, then wrap the paper around it. Once the mixture is enclosed, roll it to make a neat sausage about 25cm/10in long. Chill the roll for 30 minutes.
4 Spread the remaining biscuits over a second sheet of greaseproof paper. Unwrap the chocolate roll and use your hands to roll it over the biscuit crumbs so that it is coated evenly. Wrap the roll in greaseproof paper again, then overwrap tightly with foil, twisting the ends to seal it. Chill for at least 2 hours or overnight, until firm.
5 To serve, unwrap roll, then slice into thin rounds with a sharp knife. Serve with after-dinner coffee. Wrap leftovers well and keep in fridge for a week, or freeze for up to 1 month.

biscotti

Biscotti are dry, crisp Italian cookies that look a bit like small slices of toasted bread. The 'bis' means twice and the 'cotti' means cooked. Biscotti are perfect for dipping into coffee. In Italy they are traditionally dipped into vin santo – a golden-coloured fortified wine – as a digestif at the end of a meal.

Makes 14
Preparation 20 minutes
Cooking 30-35 minutes

275g/10oz plain flour or Italian 00
  flour, plus extra for dusting
150g/5oz caster sugar
1 tsp baking powder
2 eggs, plus 1 extra yolk
1 tsp vanilla extract
100g/4oz whole blanched almonds
icing sugar, for dusting (optional)

1 Preheat oven to 180°C/350°F/Gas 4. Put the flour, sugar, baking powder, eggs, extra yolk, vanilla extract and almonds into a bowl. Using a wooden spoon, mix the ingredients together until mixture just forms a soft dough. You may find it easier to finish mixing with your hands. The dough should be slightly soft and sticky – and not too wet or too dry – and should almost resemble homemade almond paste.
2 Tip the dough out on to a lightly floured surface and knead gently. To knead, stand with one foot in front of the other and use the heel of your hand to gently push the dough away

from you. At the same time, use your other hand to rotate the dough slightly towards you, guiding it slowly around in a circle. Repeat this action for no more than 5 minutes until the dough is smooth (overworking will give you a tough dough). Don't worry if the mixture is sticky – simply feed it with a little sprinkling of flour.

3 Lightly oil a baking sheet. Shape dough into a log and transfer to the baking sheet. Gently flatten the top of the dough with a rolling pin so you have a thickness of 2.5cm/1in. Dust with a little flour to protect the top from overbrowning. With a knife, score the dough at 2cm/³⁄₄in intervals, cutting two-thirds of the way down, to mark about 14 pieces.

4 Bake biscotti for 20 minutes until pale golden and firm to the touch.

5 Cut the biscotti mixture into pieces while still warm and soft – once cold, it is too firm to cut without shattering. Using a serrated knife, cut through the markings and arrange individual pieces, cut-side up, on the baking sheet.

6 Return the biscotti to the oven and bake for 10–15 minutes until golden, but don't let them get too brown.

7 Cool on a wire rack. Dust with icing sugar, if liked. Serve with cappuccino or hot chocolate for dunking.

Variations

There are several variations on the basic biscotti. Try using hazelnuts instead of almonds, and coat one end of the finished biscotti with melted chocolate. Melt 225g/8oz plain chocolate with a large knob of butter to cover 14 biscotti pieces – the butter prevents the chocolate from shattering when you bite into it. Let them set on the wire rack. Add 25g/1oz chopped candied peel or chopped stem ginger to this quantity of dough, or 100g/4oz chopped chocolate.

all-American chocolate chunk cookies

Makes 12
Preparation about 20 minutes
Cooking about 15 minutes

300g/11oz plain chocolate (about 55% cocoa solids)
100g/4oz bar of milk chocolate
100g/4oz light muscovado sugar
85g/3oz butter, at room temperature
100g/4oz peanut butter (crunchy is best)
1 medium egg
¹⁄₂ tsp vanilla extract
100g/4oz self-raising flour
100g/4oz large salted roasted peanuts

1 Preheat oven to 180°C/350°F/Gas 4. Chop 200g/7oz of the plain chocolate into rough, irregular chunks. Chop the milk chocolate in the same way, but keep separate.

2 Break the remaining plain chocolate into a large heatproof mixing bowl. Melt in the microwave on Medium for about 1¹⁄₂ minutes (or over a pan of simmering water). Stir the chocolate until melted, then add the sugar, butter, peanut butter, egg and vanilla, and beat until well mixed. Stir in the flour, all the milk chocolate chunks, the nuts (no need to chop) and half the plain chocolate chunks. The mixture will feel quite soft and drop easily from the spoon if you shake it.

3 Drop big spoonfuls in 12 piles on 2 or 3 baking sheets, leaving room for spreading (you may need to cook in batches). Stick the remaining chunks into the cookies (2–3 pieces in each).

4 Bake for 10–12 minutes until cookies are tinged very slightly darker around the edges. The smell will let you know they are ready. They will be soft in the middle, but crisp up as they cool. (Cook longer and you get crisper cookies.) Let cool and firm up for a few minutes on the baking sheet (they'll break up if you move them while still hot), then lift off with a wide spatula on to a cooling rack.

Acknowledgements

Features and most recipe introductions by Lewis Esson

Recipes by

Sue Ashworth
Pork fillet with roast vegetables p67

Vineet Bhatia
Mushroom biryani p92, from his restaurants Zaika, London and Bar Zaika Bazaar, London

Anne Boggiano
Spanish-style baked fish p65

Shirley Bond
Cowboy casserole p43

Lorna Brash
Butterscotch apple charlotte p119

Sarah Buenfeld
Gnocchi with two cheeses and bacon p23

Mary Cadogan
Tartiflette p10, Buttery potato cake p10, Shepherd's pie p12, Smoked salmon and haddock fish pie p15, Smoked salmon and pea frittata p15, Chicken and ham pie p29, Roasted sirloin with red onions and port gravy p54, Mint and lemon roast lamb p56, Salmon en croûte p72, Salmon and caper baklava pie p73, Pork and duck terrine p75, Red onion and goats' cheese tart p93, Courgette, tomato and basil tart p94, Cinnamon, raisin and orange rice pudding p123, Mango, banana and coconut cake p130, Chocolate salami p138

Mary Cadogan and Sarah Buenfeld
Chicken curry with chickpeas p38, Toad-in-the-hole with red onions and thyme batter p41

Mary Cadogan and Angela Nilsen
Roast pork with apples, cider vinegar and rosemary p53, Pot roasted brisket with pancetta and red wine p54, Duck with lime, ginger and honey p86

Rosemary Carroll
Ginger and lemon sponge p130

Maxine Clark
Goats' cheese and pesto cannelloni p96

Coralie Dorman
Beef en daube p59

Matthew Drennan
Butternut squash and lamb stew p62, Dark chocolate and orange cake p126

Lewis Esson
Chicken with garlic and bay leaves p38, Lamb and apricot moussaka p58, Wild mushroom tart with goats' cheese p70, Pasta with cauliflower, broccoli and chard p100, Leek and pepper pizzas p102, Toffee Brownies p129

Joanna Farrow
Chilli con carne p25, Rippled chocolate bombe p114, Mars bar mousses p117, Prune and chocolate torte p128

Ursula Ferrigno
Biscotti p138

Moyra Fraser
Greengage eggnog tart p111, Autumn plum crunch cake p132

Brian Glover
Lamb, aubergine and spinach lasagne p18, Pot roasted brisket in beer with parsnips and mushrooms p50, Lamb shanks with chickpeas and Moroccan spices p78, Garlic chicken with herbed potatoes p82, Posh beans on toast p103, Rhubarb, strawberry and cardamom crumble p112, Rhubarb and ginger pavlova p120, Mocha truffle roulade p126

Good Food Team
Gratin dauphinois p13, Ham and egg stuffed marrow p18, Ham, spinach and brie pizza p21, Spiced rice with prawns p21, Sausages with quick onion gravy and sweet potato chips p22, Moroccan lamb burgers p22, Lamb chops with root mash and onion gravy p26, Mixed mushroom and chestnut pies p28, Seafood Spaghetti p32, Tuna pasta niçoise p32, Cauli-macaroni cheese p34, Penne with blue cheese sauce p34, Rigatoni sausage bake p35, Shepherd's pie jackets p36, Cheat's moussaka p41, Spanish chicken casserole p42, Quick curried kedgeree p44, Pea, ham and potato omelette p47, Chilli baked eggs p47, Spiced lamb casserole p57, Lamb and red pepper stew p60, Quick seafood paella p63, Herby cod bake p65, Fish o'leekie p66, Mediterranean salad tarts p76, Quick beef stroganoff p83, Cheesy sweet potato and cauliflower p90, Florentine Pizza p94, Grilled vegetable couscous with halumi p98, Creamy rosemary and butternut squash pasta p98, Pear and blackberry upside down pudding p108, Cherry and almond cake p133

Fiona Hunter
Mango and passion fruit roulade p121

Mireille Johnston
Pastis p135

Theodore Kyriakou and Charles Campion
Spinach rolls with feta p90. Taken from their book *Real Greek Food* and reprinted by permission of Pavilion Books.

Sue Lawrence
Rumbledethumps p37, Potted salmon p74, Oatmeal praline ice-cream p106. All taken from her book *Scots Cooking* and reproduced by permission of Headline Book Publishing Limited.

Marie-Pierre Moine
Creamy mussels with cider and bacon p87. Taken from her book *Cuisine Grand-Mère* (Ebury Press) and reprinted by permission of the Random House Group Ltd.

Kate Moseley
Glazed chicken with potato and celeriac mash p66

Orlando Murrin
Warm summer bean and sausage salad p27, Roast rib of beef with mixed pepper and thyme crust p50, Spiced plum squares p106 , Panettone pudding p113

Vicky Musselman
All-American chocolate chunk cookies p139

Angela Nilsen
Fish cakes with tartar sauce p16, Steak and kidney pie p29, Old-fashioned and buttery potted shrimps p74, Mediterranean chicken with rocket and potato crush p86, Mushroom and goats' cheese polenta pie p97, Chive and brie omelette p101, Rhubarb cheesecake pie p109, Crêpes suzette p118, Strawberry and banana knickerbocker glories p120, Battenberg cake p135, Hot cross bun loaf p136, Comfort cottage loaf p137

Merrilees Parker
Cherry chocolate terrine p116

Adam Pasco
Parsley and walnut pesto pasta p102

Phil Vickery
Chunky chips with taleggio cheese p17, Chicken casserole with rosemary dumplings p60

Lesley Waters
Curried egg rösti p45. Taken from her book *Cooler than Chillies* and reproduced by permission of Headline Book Publishing Limited.

Ruth Watson
Soy and saké-marinated striploin of beef p55

Ann Willan
Venison and mushroom pie p70, Braised partridge with cabbage p81, Coq au vin p85

Jeni Wright
Cheese soufflé p77

Mitzie Wilson
Strawberry and cinnamon torte p123

Photographers

Marie-Louise Avery
Moroccan lamb burgers p23, Rhubarb cheesecake pie p109, Cherry chocolate terrine p116

Iain Bagwell
Cauli-macaroni cheese p34, Quick curried kedgeree p44, Pork fillet with roast vegetables p67

Martin Brigdale
Pot roasted brisket in beer with parsnips and mushrooms p51, Lamb shanks with chickpeas and Moroccan spices p79

Linda Burgess
Lamb, aubergine and spinach lasagne p18, Strawberry and cinnamon torte p122, Mocha truffle roulade p127

Jean Cazals
Salmon and caper baklava pie p73, Pastis p114, Chocolate salami p138

Tim de Winter
Buttery potato cake p11

Ken Field
Spiced rice with prawns p21, Tuna pasta niçoise p33, Chicken with garlic and bay leaves p39, Herby cod bake p65, Posh beans on toast p103, Greengage and eggnog tart p110

Good Food Picture Library
Cheat's moussaka p41

Tim Imrie
Cherry and almond cake p133, All-American chocolate chunk cookies p139

David Munns
Rigatoni sausage bake p35, Cowboy casserole p43, Lamb and apricot moussaka p58, Spanish-style baked fish p64, Glazed chicken with potato and celeriac mash p66, Mediterranean salad tarts p76, Creamy mussels with cider and bacon p87, Pasta with cauliflower, broccoli and chard p100, Parsley and walnut pesto pasta p102, Leek and pepper pizzas p103, Spiced plum squares p107, Butterscotch apple charlotte p119, Mango and passion fruit roulade p121

Michael Paul
Toffee brownies p129

Nick Pope
Smoked salmon and haddock fish pie p14, Hot cross bun loaf p136

Simon Smith
Roast rib of beef with mixed pepper and thyme crust p48

Martin Thompson
Soy and saké-marinated striploin of beef p55

Roger Stowell
Gratin dauphinois p13, Chunky chips with taleggio cheese p17, Ham and egg stuffed marrow p19, Ham, spinach and brie pizza p20, Sausages with quick onion gravy and sweet potato chips p22, Lamb chops with root mash and onion gravy p26, Mixed mushroom and chestnut pies p28, Seafood spaghetti p30, Penne with blue cheese sauce p35, Shepherd's pie jackets p36, Spanish chicken casserole p42, Curried egg rösti p45, Pea, ham and potato omelette p46, Roast pork with apples, cider vinegar and rosemary p52, Pot roasted brisket with pancetta and red wine p54, Spiced lamb casserole p57, Beef en daube p59, Chicken casserole with rosemary dumplings p61, Quick seafood paella p63, Fish o'leekie p67, Wild mushroom tart with goats' cheese p70, Venison and mushroom pie p71, Cheese soufflé p77, Braised partridge with cabbage p80, Garlic chicken with herbed potatoes p82, Quick beef stroganoff p83, Duck with lime, ginger and honey p87, Cheesy sweet potato and cauliflower p91, Florentine pizza p94, Creamy rosemary and butternut squash pasta p99, Chive and brie omelette p101, Pear and blackberry upside down pudding p108, Mango, banana and coconut cake p130, Comfort cottage loaf p137

Ian Wallace
Panettone pudding p113, Strawberry and banana knickerbocker glories p120

Simon Walton
Gnocchi with two cheeses and bacon p23

Philip Webb
Warm summer bean and sausage salad p27, Mediterranean chicken with rocket and potato crush p86, Spinach rolls with feta p88, Goats' cheese and pesto cannelloni p96, Rhubarb, strawberry and cardamom crumble p112, Rippled chocolate bombe p115, Mars bar mousses p117, Rhubarb and ginger pavlova p121, Dark chocolate and orange cake p124, Prune and chocolate torte p128, Autumn plum crunch cake p132

Simon Wheeler
Tartiflette p8, Shepherd's pie p12, Smoked salmon and pea frittata p15, Fish cakes with tartar sauce p16, Chilli con carne p24, Steak and kidney pie p29, Rumbledethumps p37, Chicken curry with chickpeas p38, Toad-in-the-hole with red onions and thyme batter p40, Salmon en croûte p72, Potted salmon p74, Old-fashioned and buttery potted shrimps p74, Pork and duck terrine p75, Coq au vin p84, Mushroom biryani p92, Red onion and goats' cheese tart p93, Courgette, tomato and basil tart p95, Oatmeal praline ice cream p104, Crêpes suzette p118

Geoff Wilkinson
Chicken and ham pie p29, Roasted sirloin with red onions and port gravy p54, Mint and lemon roast lamb p56, Mushroom and goats' cheese polenta pie p97, Ginger and lemon sponge p131, Biscotti p139

Tim Young
Butternut squash and spiced lamb stew p62

While every effort has been made to trace and acknowledge all copyright holders, we would like to apologize should there be any errors or omissions.

Index